FOUR CHORD SONGS

ISBN 978-1-5400-0521-2

Visit Hal Leonard Online at
www.halleonard.com

Contact Us:
Hal Leonard
7777 West Bluemound Road
Milwaukee, WI 53213
Email: info@halleonard.com

In Europe contact:
Hal Leonard Europe Limited
42 Wigmore Street
Marylebone, London, W1U 2RN
Email: info@halleonardeurope.com

In Australia contact:
Hal Leonard Australia Pty. Ltd.
4 Lentara Court
Cheltenham, Victoria, 3192 Australia
Email: info@halleonard.com.au

Welcome to the *Super Easy Songbook* series!

This unique collection will help you play your favorite songs quickly and easily. Here's how it works:

- Play the simplified melody with your right hand. Letter names appear inside each note to assist you.

- There are no key signatures to worry about! If a sharp ♯ or flat ♭ is needed, it is shown beside the note each time.

- There are no page turns, so your hands never have to leave the keyboard.

- If two notes are connected by a tie ⌣, hold the first note for the combined number of beats. (The second note does not show a letter name since it is not re-struck.)

- Add basic chords with your left hand using the provided keyboard diagrams. Chord voicings have been carefully chosen to minimize hand movement.

- The left-hand rhythm is up to you, and chord notes can be played together or separately. Be creative!

- If the chords sound muddy, move your left hand an octave* higher. If this gets in the way of playing the melody, move your right hand an octave higher as well.

  * *An octave spans eight notes. If your starting note is C, the next C to the right is an octave higher.*

ALSO AVAILABLE

Hal Leonard Student Keyboard Guide HL00296039

Key Stickers HL00100016

Addicted to Love

Words and Music by
Robert Palmer

mune ___ to the stuff, oh yeah. ___ It's clos -

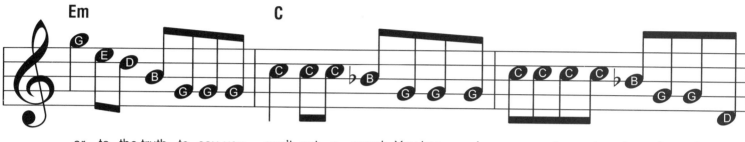

er to the truth to say you can't get e - nough. You know you're gon-na have to face it, you're ad -

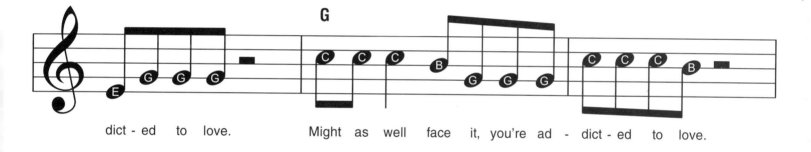

dict - ed to love. Might as well face it, you're ad - dict - ed to love.

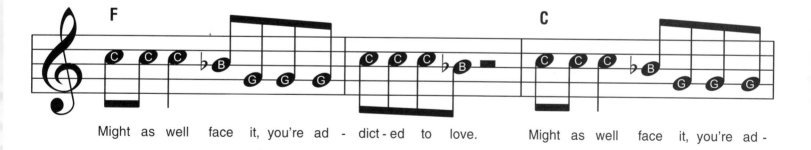

Might as well face it, you're ad - dict - ed to love. Might as well face it, you're ad -

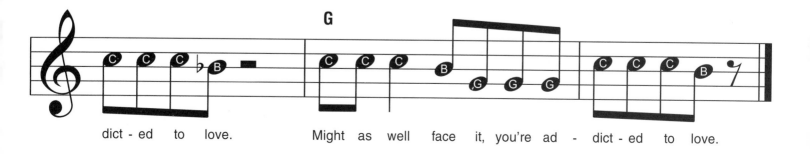

dict - ed to love. Might as well face it, you're ad - dict - ed to love.

Beast of Burden

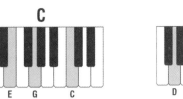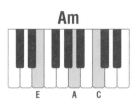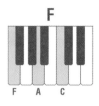

Words and Music by Mick Jagger
and Keith Richards

Moderate Rock

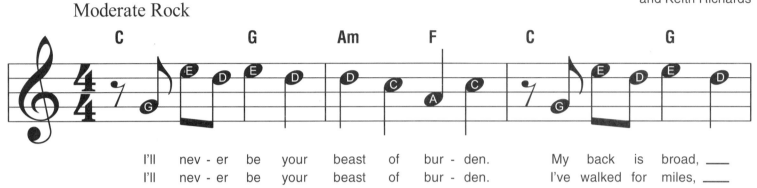

I'll nev-er be your beast of bur-den. My back is broad, ___
I'll nev-er be your beast of bur-den. I've walked for miles, ___

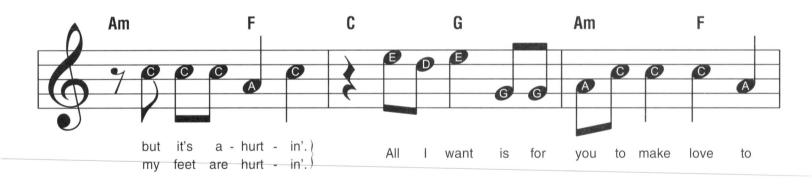

but it's a-hurt-in'.
my feet are hurt-in'. All I want is for you to make love to

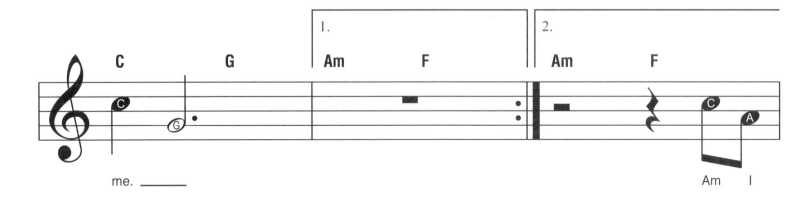

me. ___

Am I

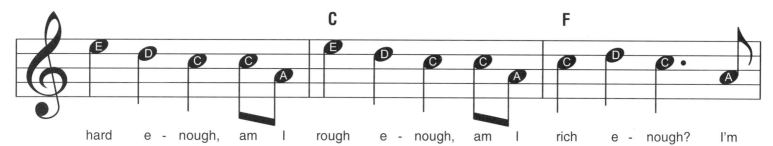

hard e - nough, am I rough e - nough, am I rich e - nough? I'm

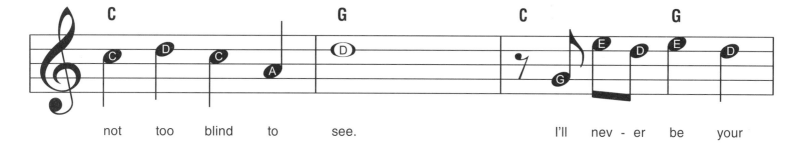

not too blind to see. I'll nev - er be your

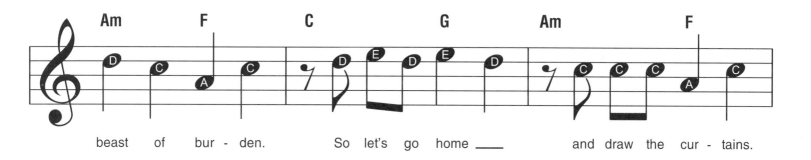

beast of bur - den. So let's go home _____ and draw the cur - tains.

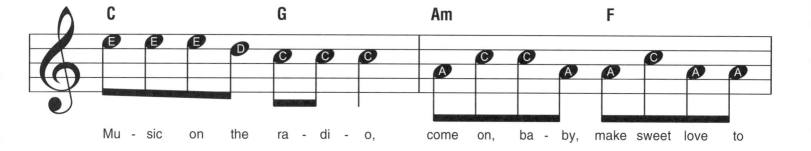

Mu - sic on the ra - di - o, come on, ba - by, make sweet love to

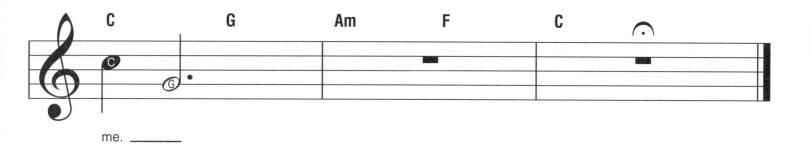

me. _____

Blowin' in the Wind

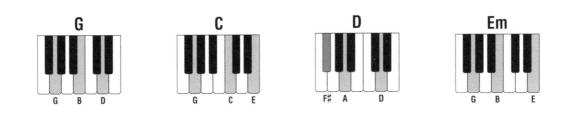

Words and Music by
Bob Dylan

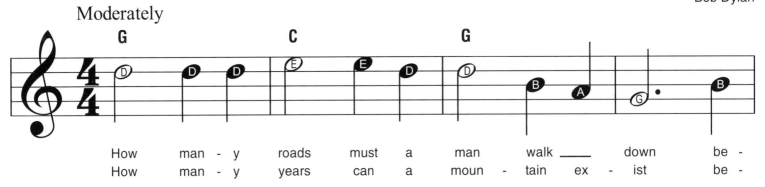

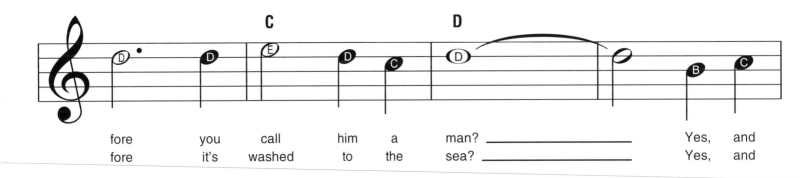

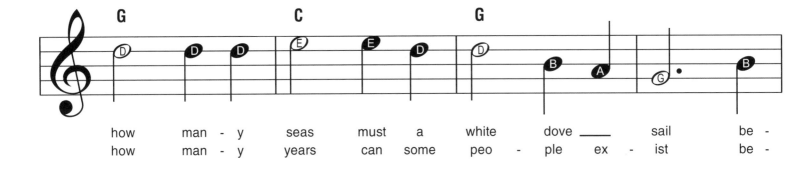

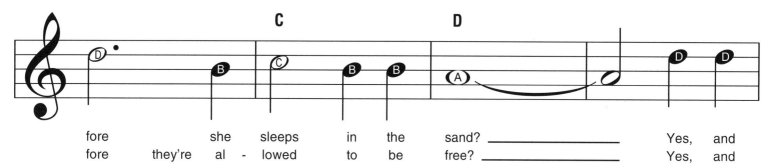

fore   she   sleeps   in   the   sand? _____ Yes,   and
fore   they're   al - lowed   to   be   free? _____ Yes,   and

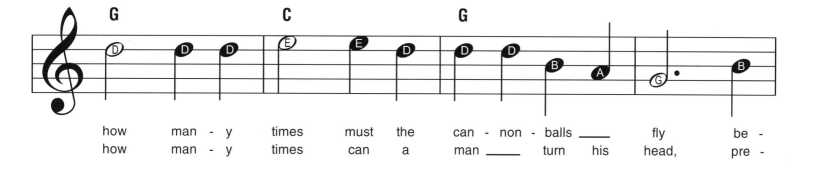

how   man - y   times   must   the   can - non - balls ____ fly   be -
how   man - y   times   can   a   man ____ turn   his   head,   pre -

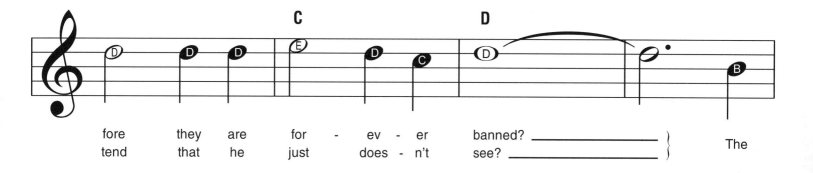

fore   they   are   for - ev - er   banned? _____ }   The
tend   that   he   just   does - n't   see? _____ }

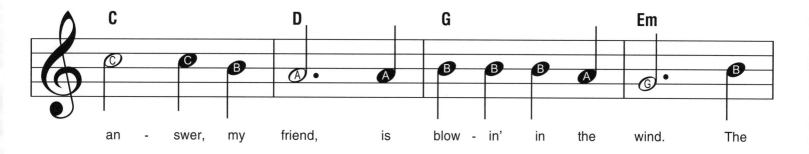

an - swer, my   friend,   is   blow - in'   in   the   wind.   The

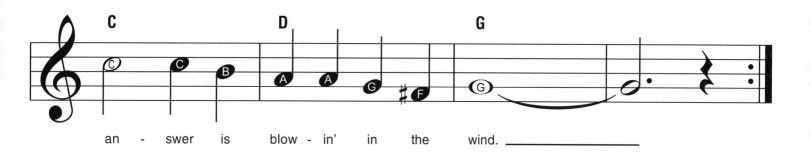

an - swer   is   blow - in'   in   the   wind. _____

The Boys of Summer

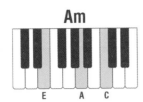 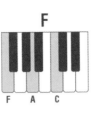 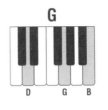 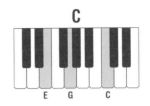

Words and Music by Mike Campbell
and Don Henley

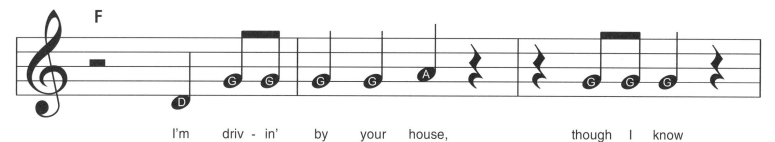

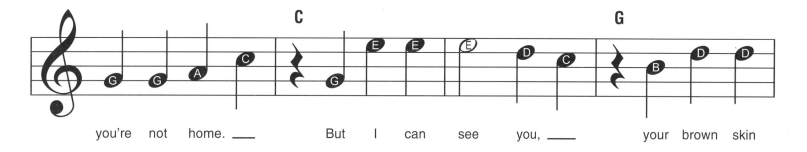

I'm driv - in' by your house, though I know

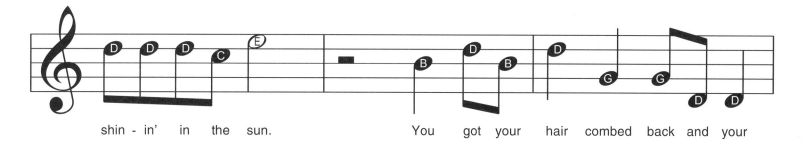

you're not home. ___ But I can see you, ___ your brown skin

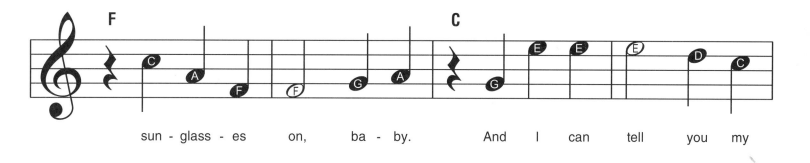

shin - in' in the sun. You got your hair combed back and your

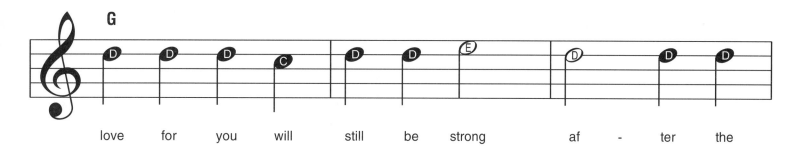

sun - glass - es on, ba - by. And I can tell you my

love for you will still be strong af - ter the

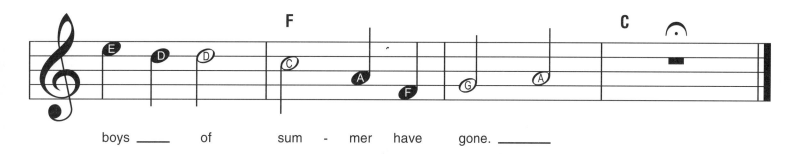

boys ___ of sum - mer have gone. ___

Breathe

Words and Music by Holly Lamar
and Stephanie Bentley

Brown Eyed Girl

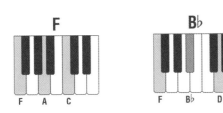
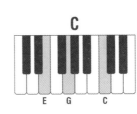

Words and Music by
Van Morrison

Moderately fast

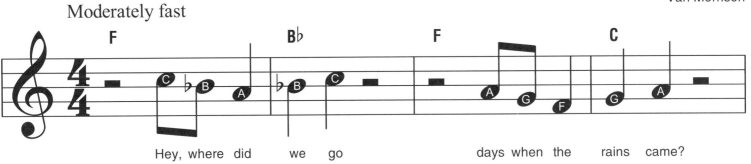

Hey, where did we go days when the rains came?

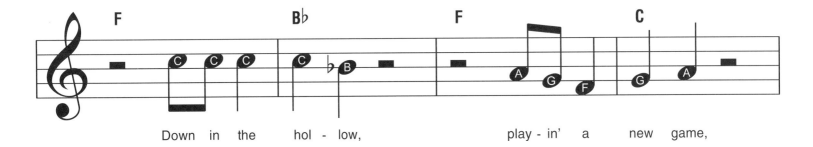

Down in the hol - low, play - in' a new game,

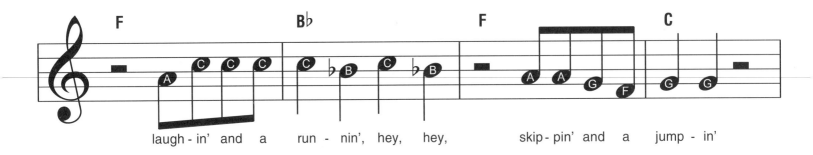

laugh - in' and a run - nin', hey, hey, skip - pin' and a jump - in'

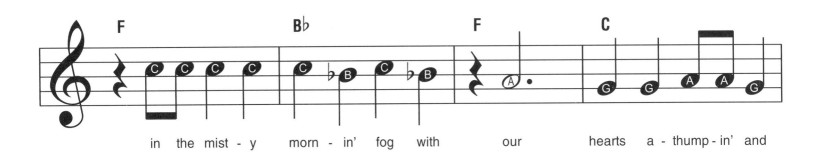

in the mist - y morn - in' fog with our hearts a - thump - in' and

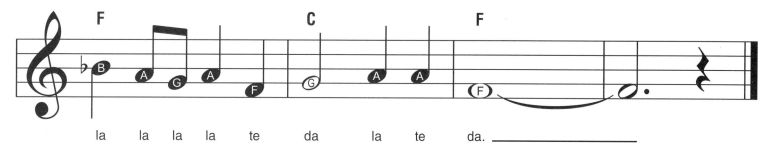

Careless Whisper

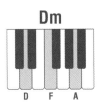
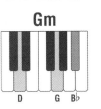
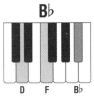
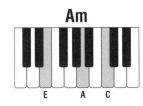

Words and Music by George Michael
and Andrew Ridgeley

Moderately

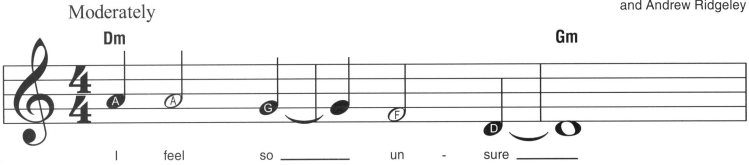

I feel so _____ un - sure _____

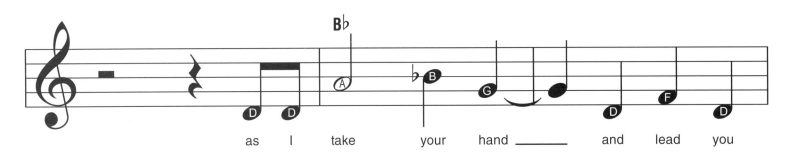

as I take your hand _____ and lead you

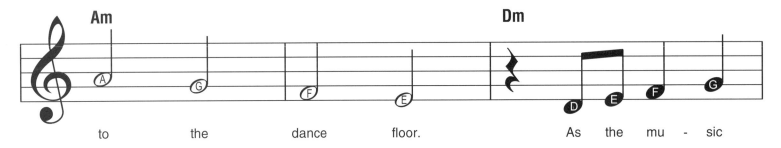

to the dance floor. As the mu - sic

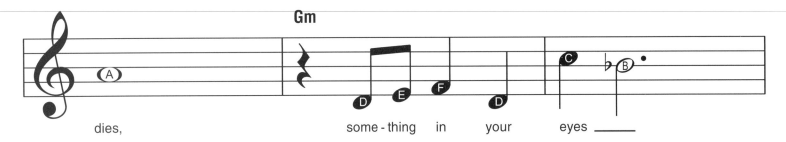

dies, some - thing in your eyes _____

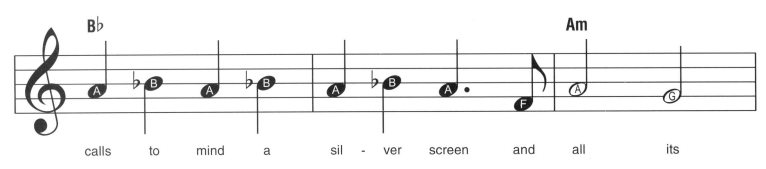

calls to mind a sil - ver screen and all its

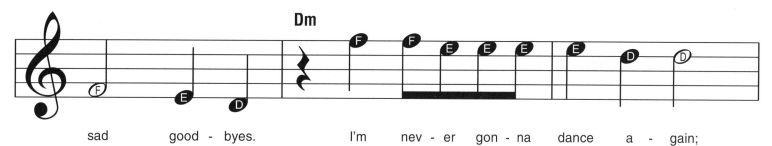

sad good-byes. I'm nev-er gon-na dance a-gain;

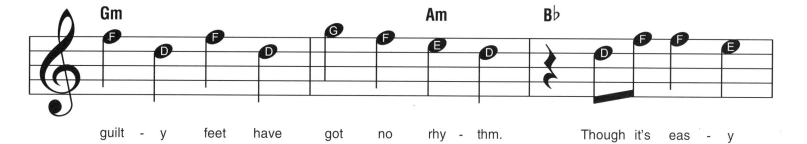

guilt-y feet have got no rhy-thm. Though it's eas-y

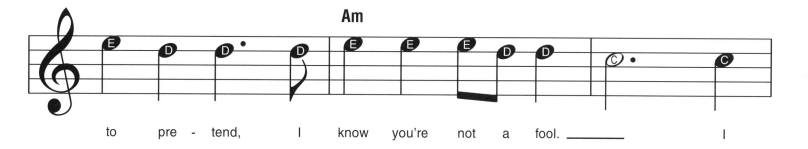

to pre-tend, I know you're not a fool. _____ I

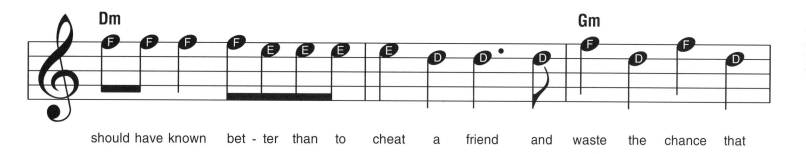

should have known bet-ter than to cheat a friend and waste the chance that

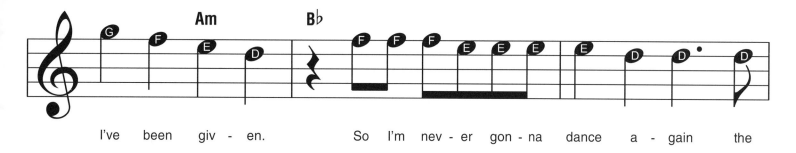

I've been giv-en. So I'm nev-er gon-na dance a-gain the

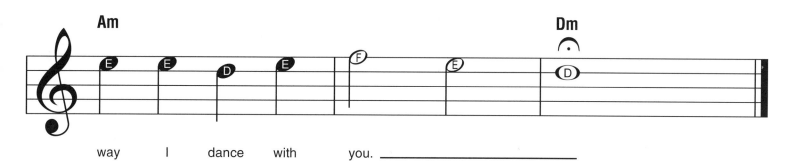

way I dance with you. _____

Come Together

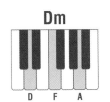 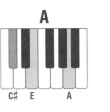 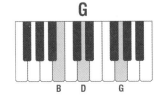 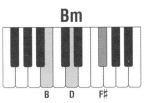

Words and Music by John Lennon
and Paul McCartney

21

Despacito

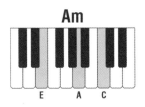
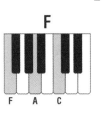
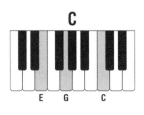
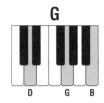

Words and Music by Luis Fonsi,
Erika Ender, Justin Bieber,
Jason Boyd, Marty James Garton
and Ramón Ayala

Moderate Latin beat
(no chord)

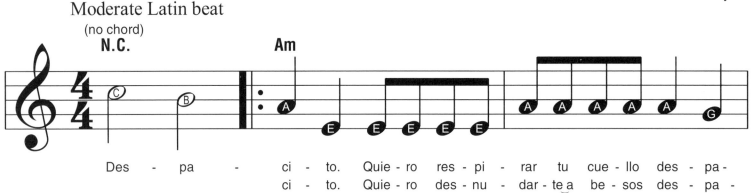

Des - pa - ci - to. Quie-ro res-pi - rar tu cue-llo des - pa -
ci - to. Quie-ro des-nu - dar-te a be - sos des - pa -

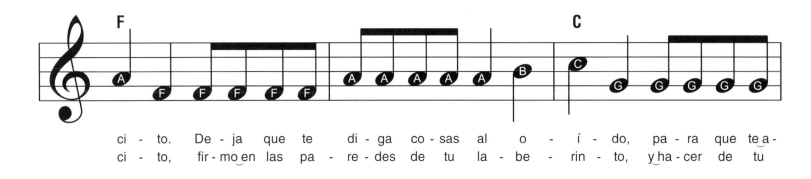

ci - to. De - ja que te di - ga co-sas al o - í - do, pa - ra que te a -
ci - to, fir - mo en las pa - re - des de tu la - be - rin - to, y ha-cer de tu

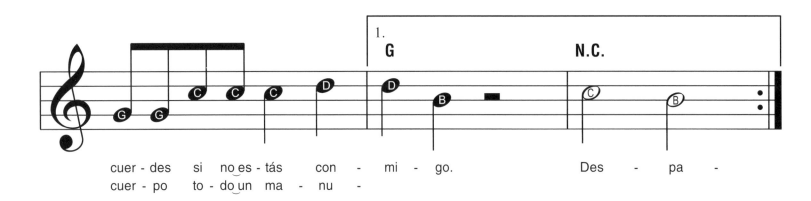

cuer - des si no es - tás con - mi - go. Des - pa -
cuer - po to - do un ma - nu -

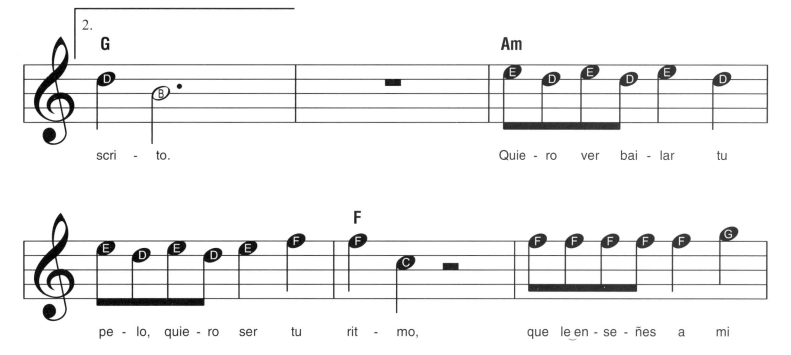

scri - to.
Quie - ro ver bai - lar tu

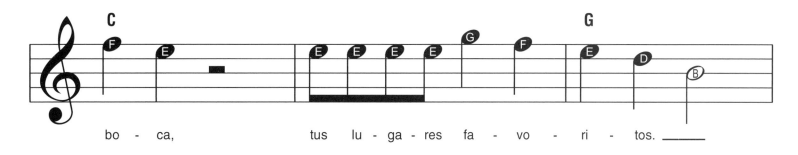

pe - lo, quie - ro ser tu rit - mo,
que le en - se - ñes a mi

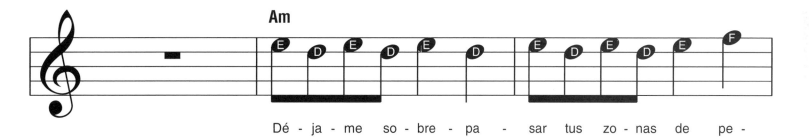

bo - ca,
tus lu - ga - res fa - vo - ri - tos. _____

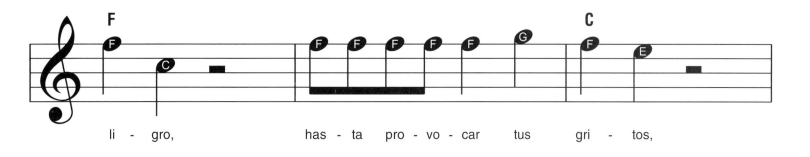

Dé - ja - me so - bre - pa - sar tus zo - nas de pe -

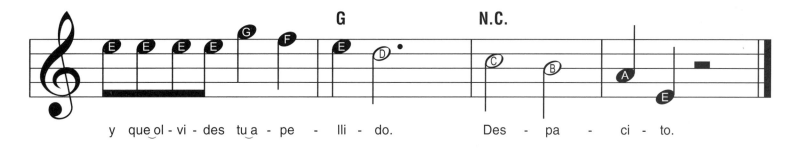

li - gro,
has - ta pro - vo - car tus gri - tos,

y que ol - vi - des tu a - pe - lli - do.
Des - pa - ci - to.

Drift Away

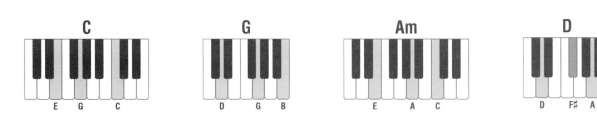

Words and Music by
Mentor Williams

Moderately

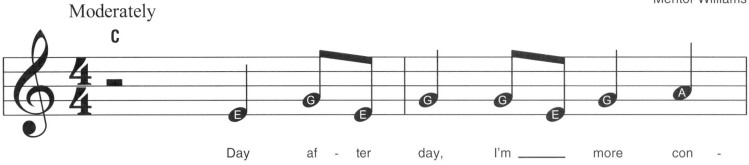

Day af - ter day, I'm _____ more con -

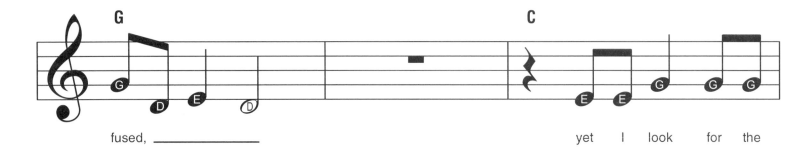

fused, _____ yet I look for the

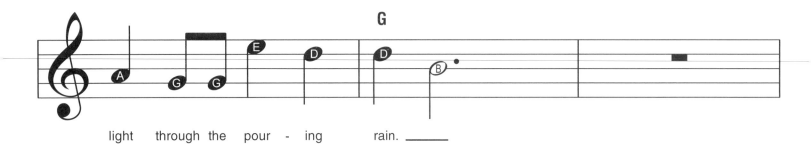

light through the pour - ing rain. _____

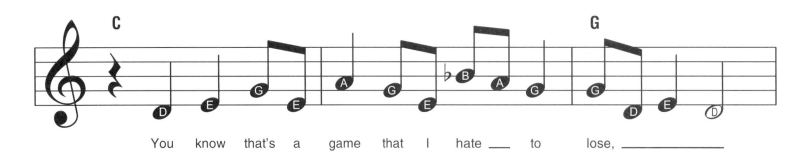

You know that's a game that I hate ___ to lose, _____

and I'm feel-ing the strain. _____

Ain't it a shame? Oh, give me the beat, boys, and

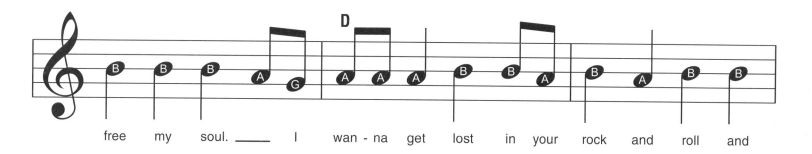

free my soul. _____ I wan-na get lost in your rock and roll and

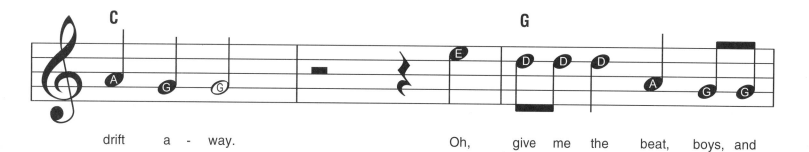

drift a - way. Oh, give me the beat, boys, and

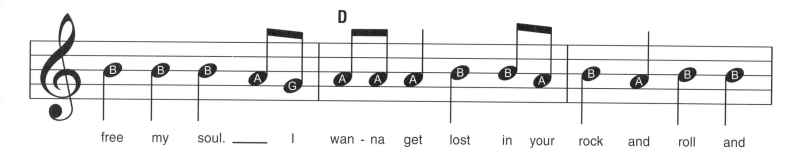

free my soul. _____ I wan-na get lost in your rock and roll and

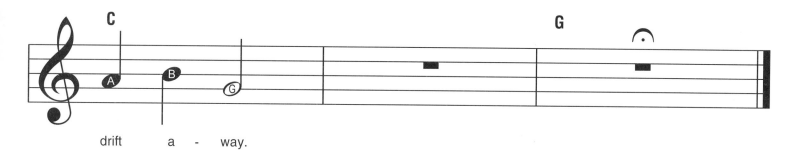

drift a - way.

Falling Slowly
from the Motion Picture ONCE

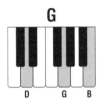

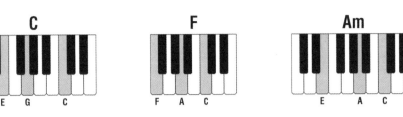

Words and Music by Glen Hansard
and Marketa Irglova

Slowly

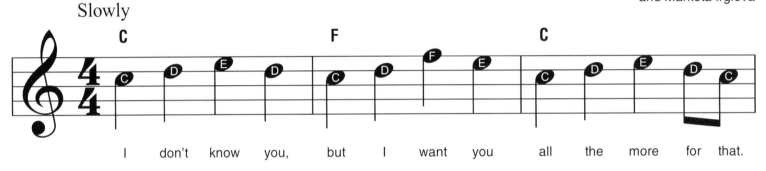

I don't know you, but I want you all the more for that.

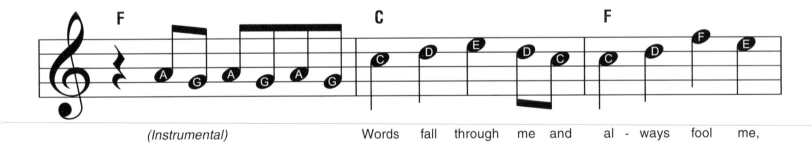

(Instrumental)   Words fall through me and al - ways fool me,

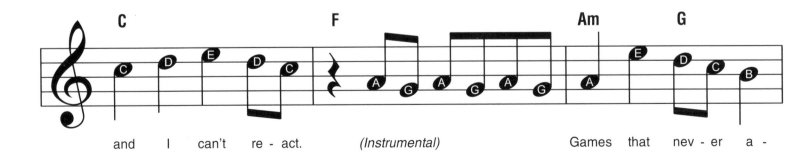

and I can't re - act.   (Instrumental)   Games that nev - er a -

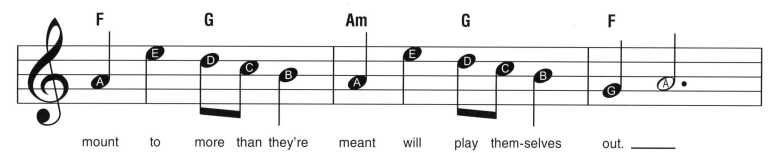

mount   to   more than they're   meant   will   play them-selves   out. _____

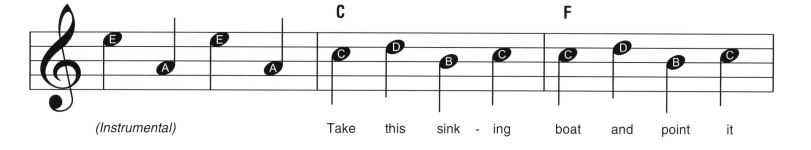

(Instrumental)   Take   this   sink - ing   boat   and   point   it

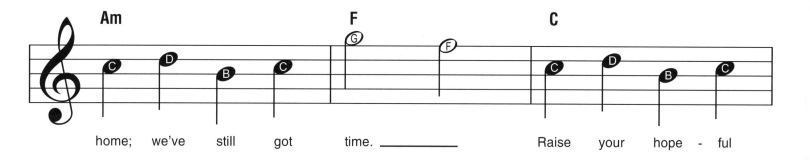

home;   we've   still   got   time. _____   Raise   your   hope - ful

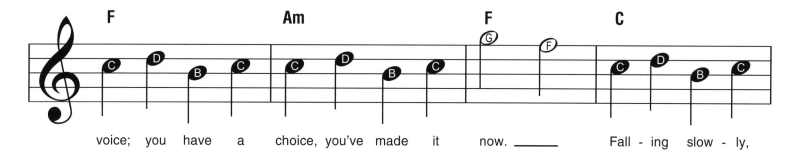

voice;   you   have   a   choice, you've   made   it   now. _____   Fall - ing   slow - ly,

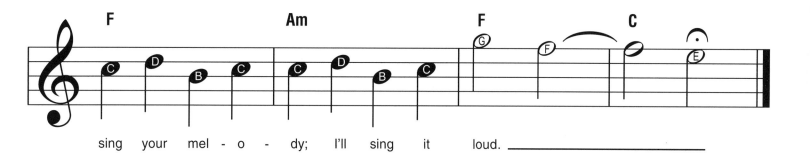

sing   your   mel - o - dy;   I'll   sing   it   loud. _____

Get Lucky

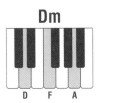
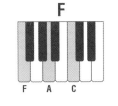
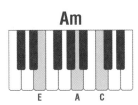
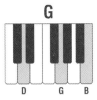

Words and Music by Thomas Bangalter,
Guy Manuel Homem Christo, Nile Rodgers
and Pharrell Williams

Moderate Dance beat
(no chord)

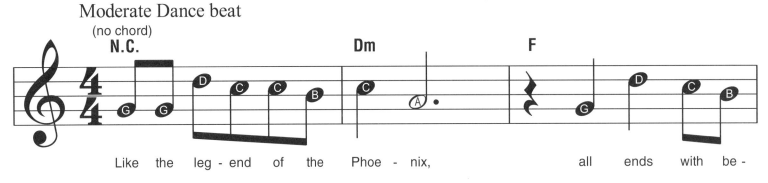

Like the leg-end of the Phoe-nix, all ends with be-

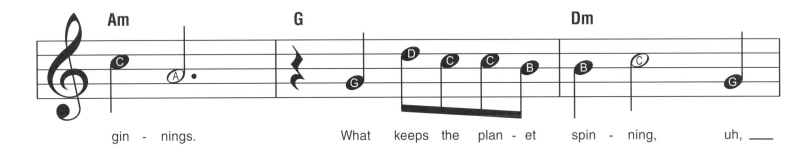

gin-nings. What keeps the plan-et spin-ning, uh, ___

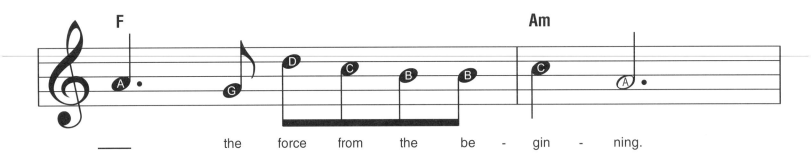

___ the force from the be-gin-ning.

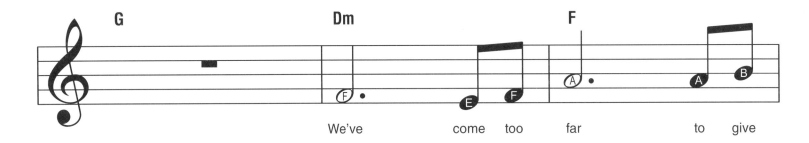

We've come too far to give

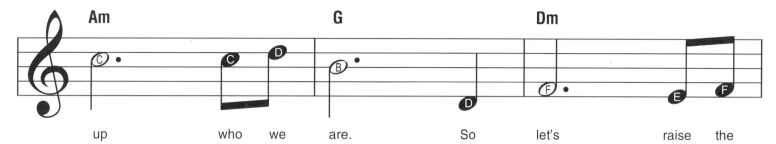

up   who we are.   So   let's   raise the

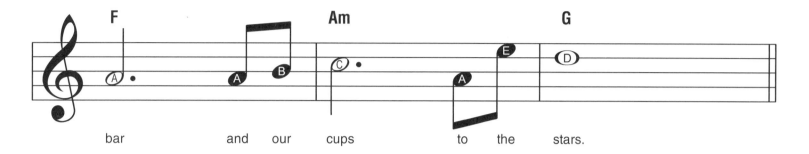

bar   and our cups   to the stars.

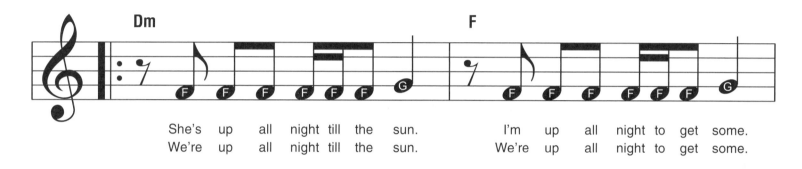

She's up all night till the sun.   I'm up all night to get some.
We're up all night till the sun.   We're up all night to get some.

She's up all night for good fun.   I'm up all night to get luck - y.
We're up all night for good fun.   We're up all night to get luck - y.

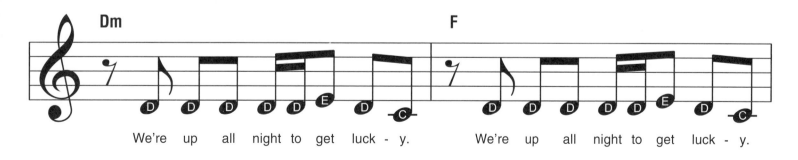

We're up all night to get luck - y.   We're up all night to get luck - y.

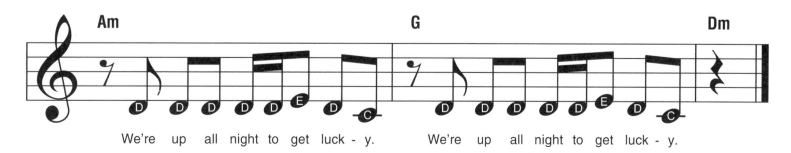

We're up all night to get luck - y.   We're up all night to get luck - y.

Good Riddance
(Time of Your Life)

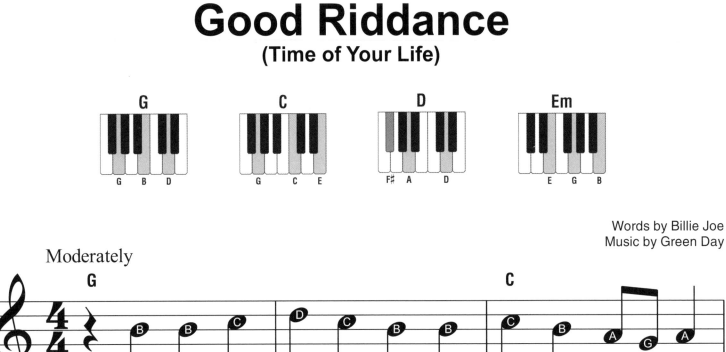

Words by Billie Joe
Music by Green Day

An - oth - er turn - ing point, a fork stuck in the ___
So, take the pho - to - graphs and still frames in your ___

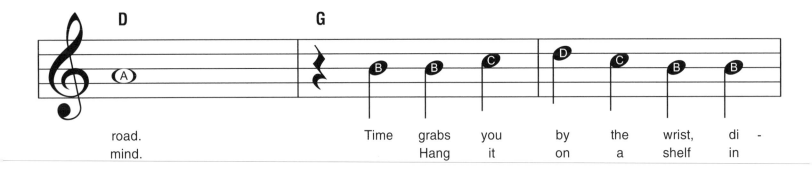

road.
mind.

Time grabs you by the wrist, di -
Hang it on on a shelf in

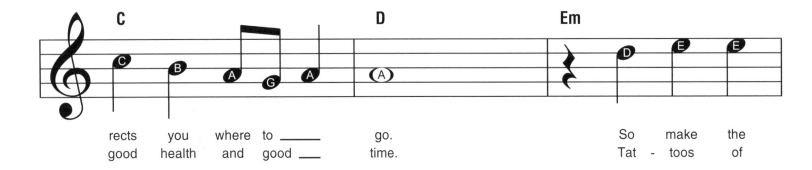

rects you where to ___ go.
good health and good ___ time.

So make the
Tat - toos of

best of this test and don't ask why. _____
mem - 'ries and dead ____ skin on trial. _____

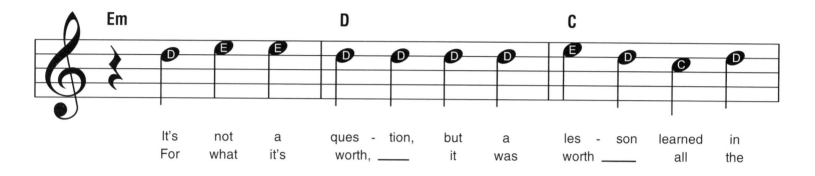

It's not a ques - tion, but a les - son learned in
For what it's worth, ____ it was worth ____ all the

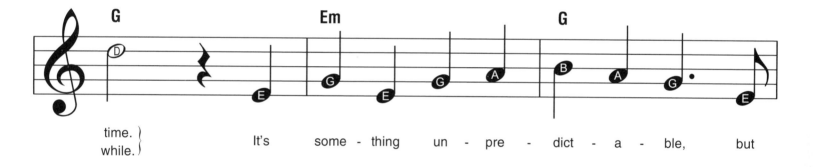

time. }
while. }
It's some - thing un - pre - dict - a - ble, but

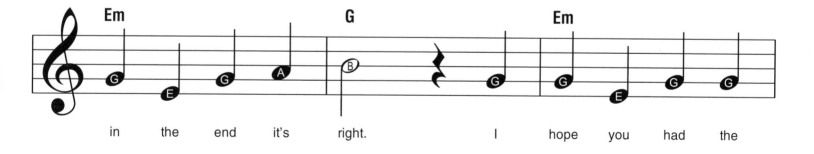

in the end it's right. I hope you had the

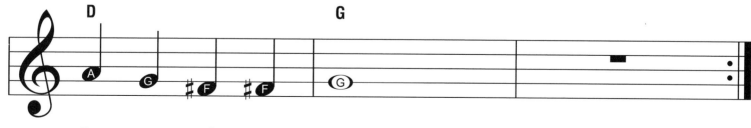

time ____ of your life.

Have You Ever Seen the Rain?

Words and Music by
John Fogerty

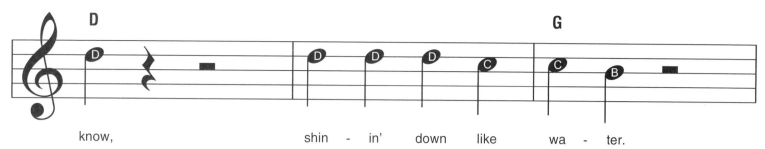

know,   shin - in' down like   wa - ter.

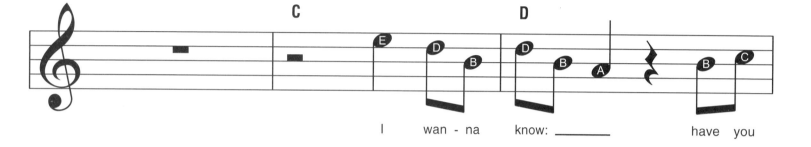

I wan - na   know: _____   have you

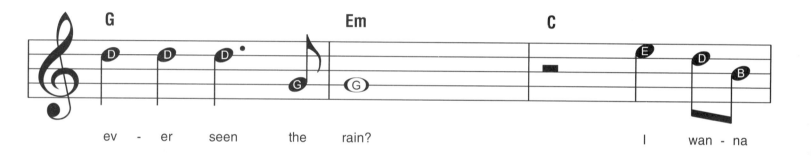

ev - er seen the rain?   I wan - na

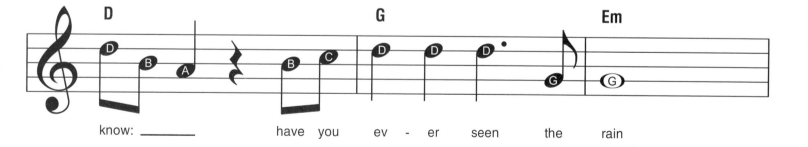

know: _____   have you ev - er seen the rain

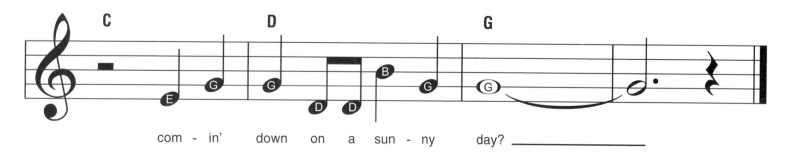

com - in' down on a sun - ny day? _____

Hello

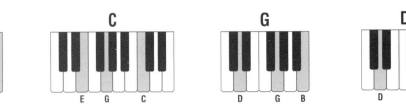

Words and Music by Adele Adkins
and Greg Kurstin

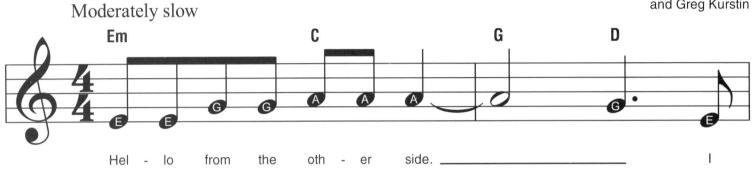

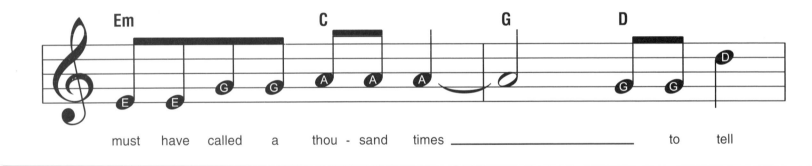

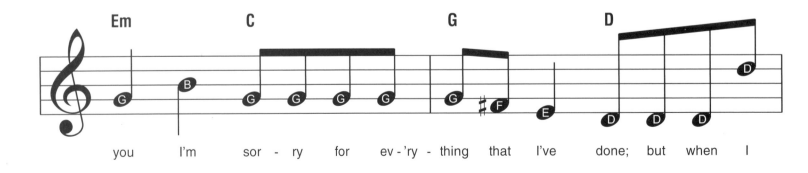

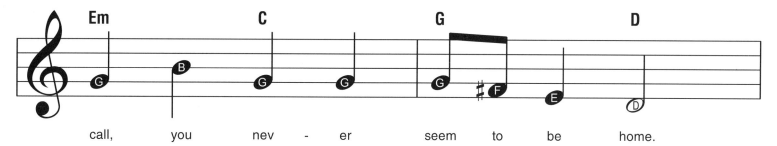

call, you nev - er seem to be home.

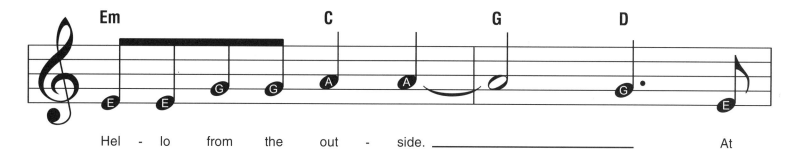

Hel - lo from the out - side. _____ At

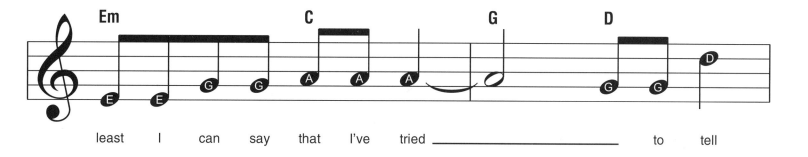

least I can say that I've tried _____ to tell

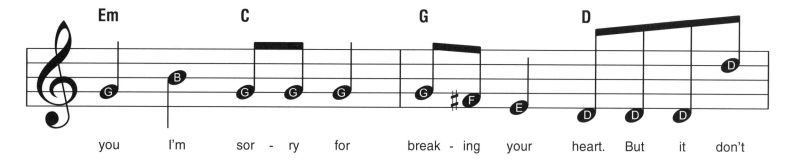

you I'm sor - ry for break - ing your heart. But it don't

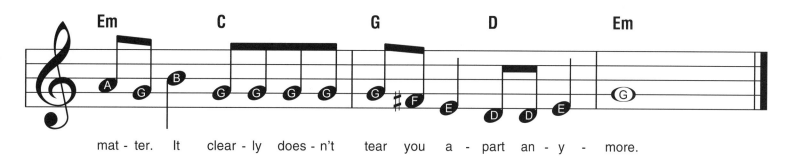

mat - ter. It clear - ly does - n't tear you a - part an - y - more.

Hey, Soul Sister

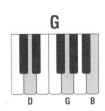 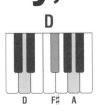 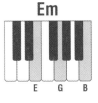 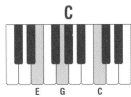

Words and Music by Pat Monahan,
Espen Lind and Amund Bjørklund

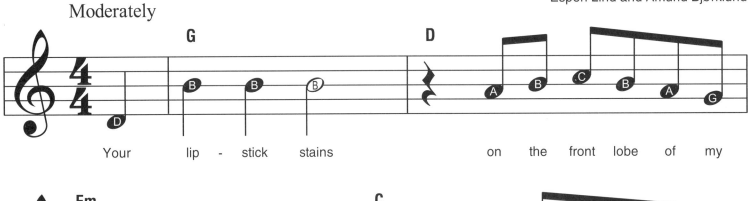

Your lip - stick stains on the front lobe of my

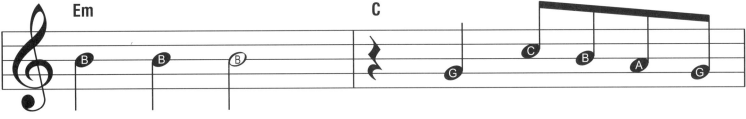

left - side brains. I knew I would - n't for -

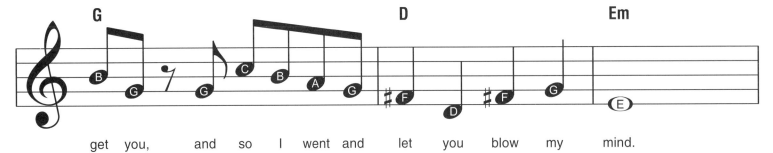

get you, and so I went and let you blow my mind.

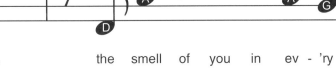

Your sweet moon - beam, the smell of you in ev - 'ry

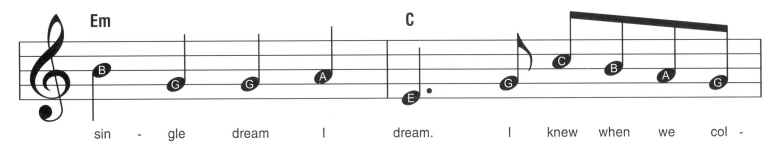

sin - gle dream I dream. I knew when we col -

How to Save a Life

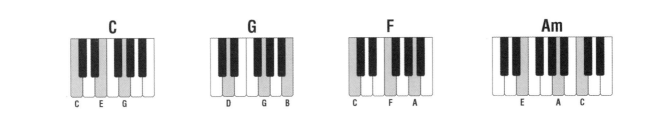

Words and Music by Joseph King
and Isaac Slade

Moderately

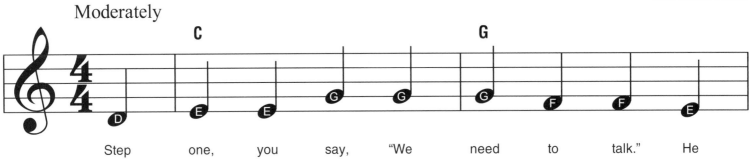

Step one, you say, "We need to talk." He

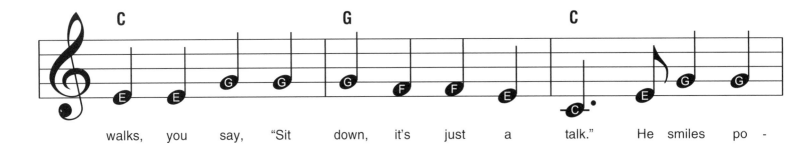

walks, you say, "Sit down, it's just a talk." He smiles po -

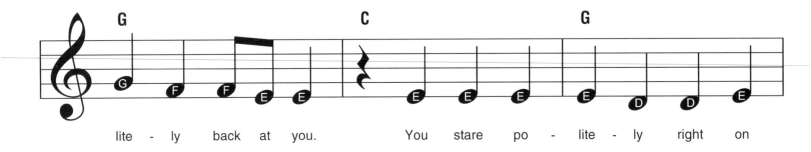

lite - ly back at you. You stare po - lite - ly right on

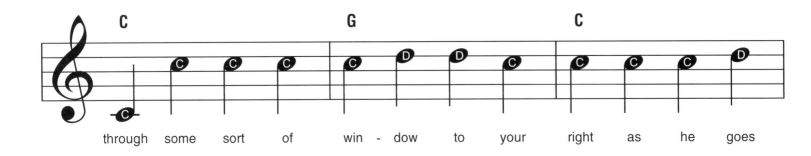

through some sort of win - dow to your right as he goes

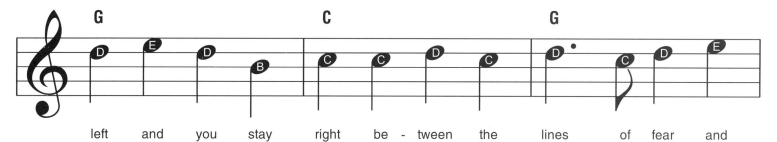

left and you stay right be - tween the lines of fear and

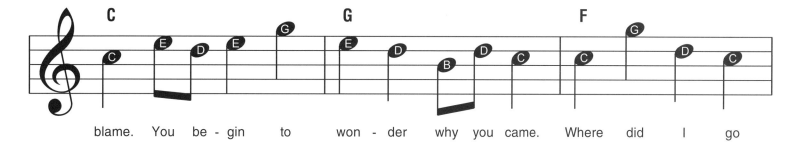

blame. You be - gin to won - der why you came. Where did I go

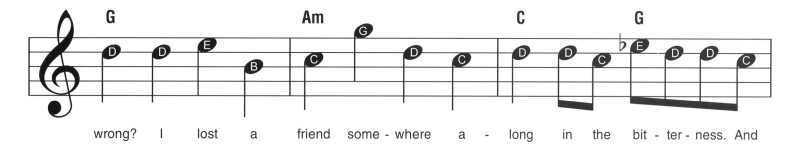

wrong? I lost a friend some - where a - long in the bit - ter - ness. And

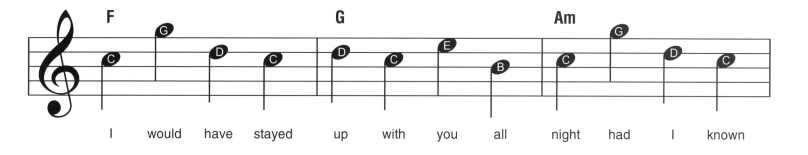

I would have stayed up with you all night had I known

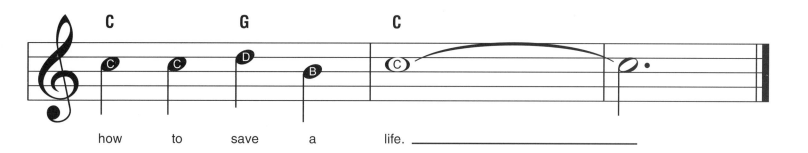

how to save a life. ___

I Saw Her Standing There

Words and Music by John Lennon
and Paul McCartney

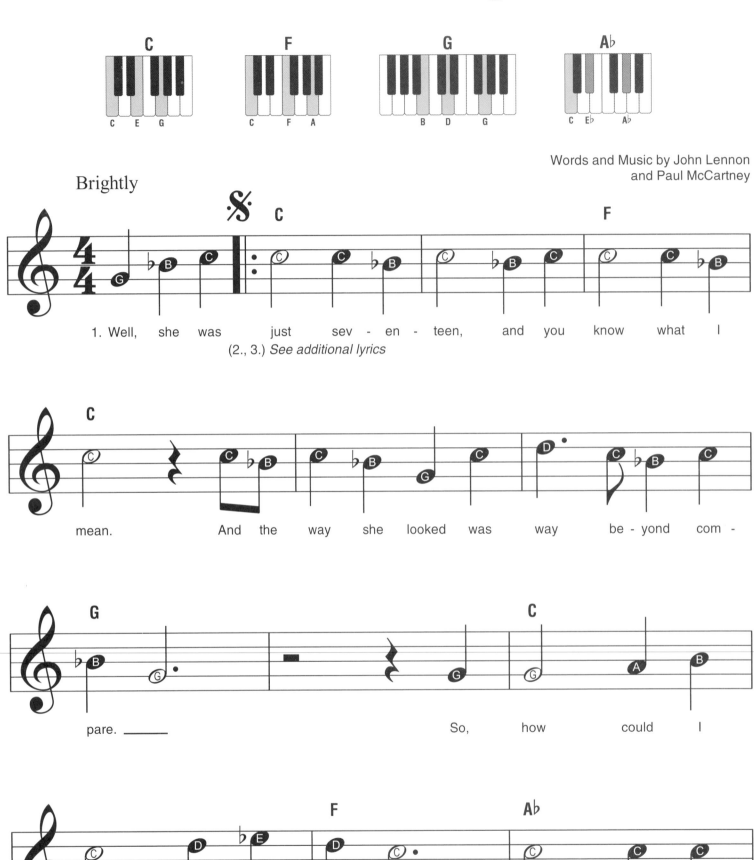

1. Well, she was just sev - en - teen, and you know what I
(2., 3.) *See additional lyrics*

mean. And the way she looked was way be - yond com -

pare. _____ So, how could I

dance with an - oth - er, ooh, when I

Additional Lyrics

2. Well, she looked at me, and I, I could see
   That before too long, I'd fall in love with her.
   She wouldn't dance with another, ooh,
   When I saw her standing there.

3. Well, we danced through the night
   And we held each other tight,
   And before too long, I fell in love with her.
   Now, I'll never dance with another, ooh,
   Since I saw her standing there.

I'll Be

Words and Music by
Edwin McCain

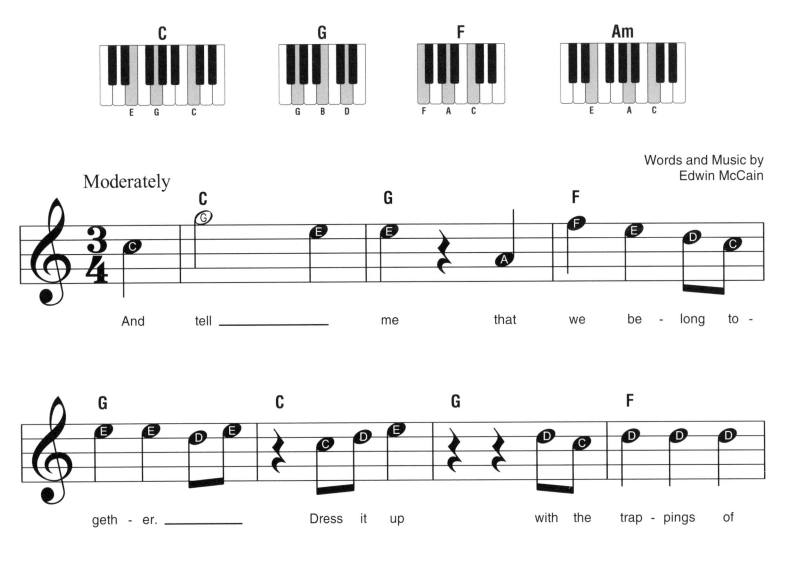

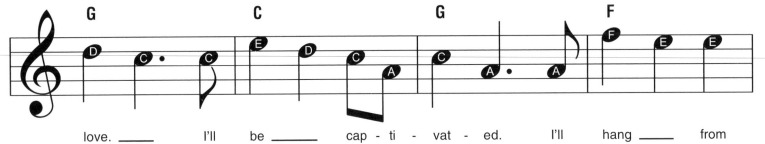

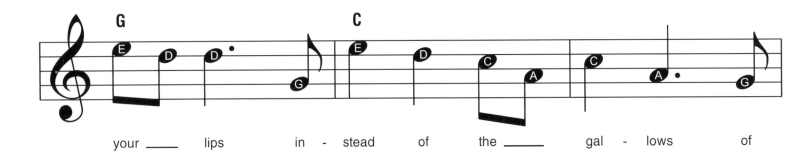

And tell _____ me that we be - long to -

geth - er. _____ Dress it up with the trap - pings of

love. ____ I'll be ____ cap - ti - vat - ed. I'll hang ____ from

your ____ lips in - stead of the ____ gal - lows of

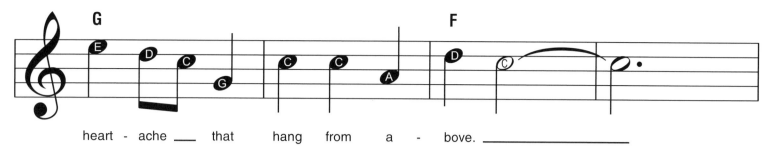

heart - ache ___ that hang from a - bove. _____

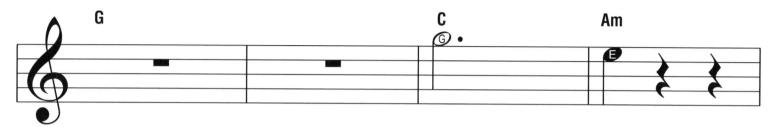

I'll   be

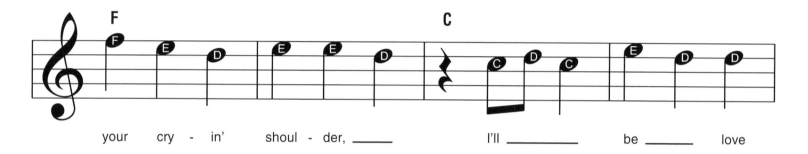

your cry - in' shoul - der, _____ I'll _____ be _____ love

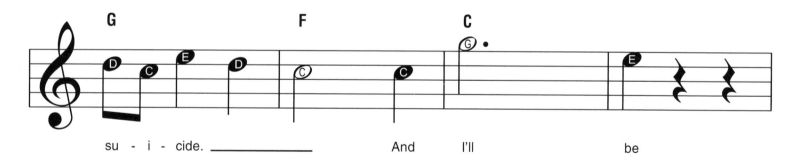

su - i - cide. _____ And I'll   be

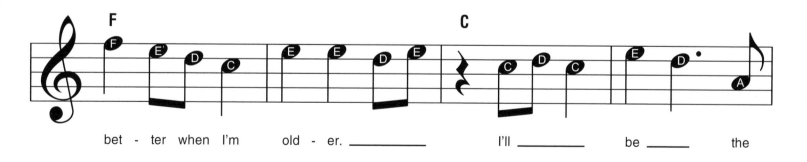

bet - ter when I'm old - er. _____ I'll _____ be _____ the

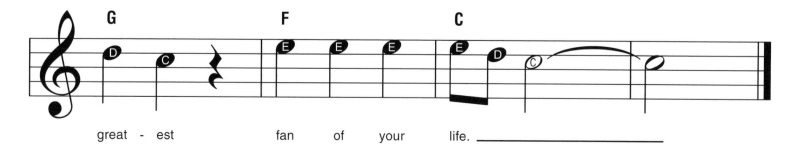

great - est   fan of your life. _____

I'm a Believer

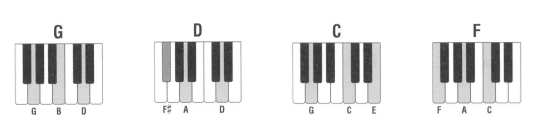

Words and Music by
Neil Diamond

Moderately fast

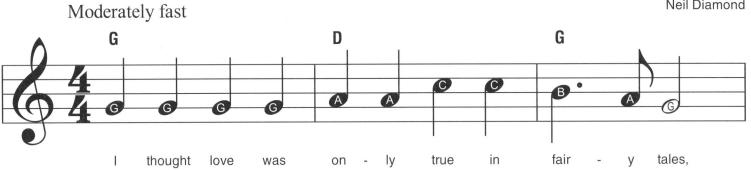

I thought love was on - ly true in fair - y tales,

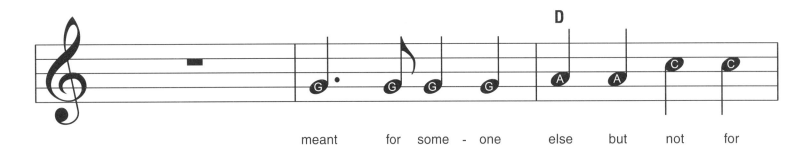

meant for some - one else but not for

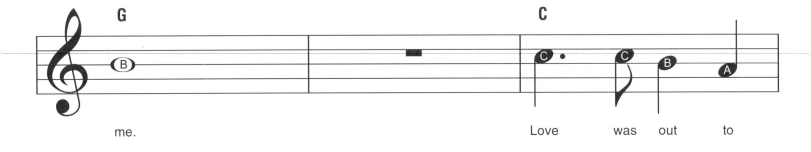

me.   Love was out to

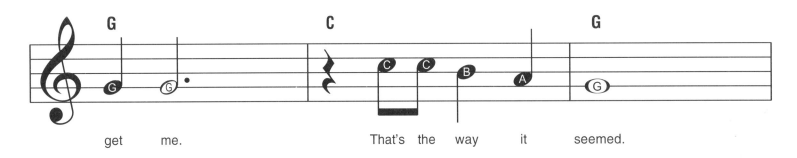

get me.   That's the way it seemed.

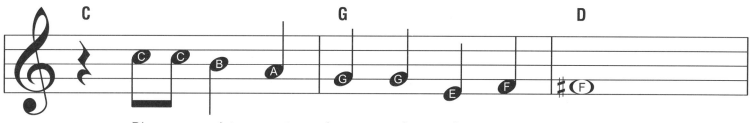

C   G   D

Dis - ap - point - ment haunt - ed all my dreams.

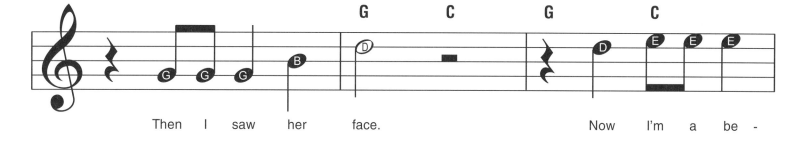

G   C   G   C

Then I saw her face.   Now I'm a be -

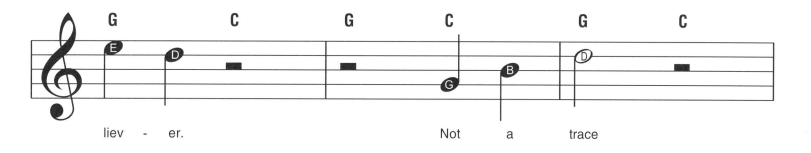

G   C   G   C   G   C

liev - er.   Not a trace

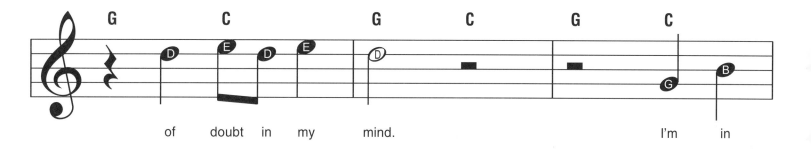

G   C   G   C   G   C

of doubt in my mind.   I'm in

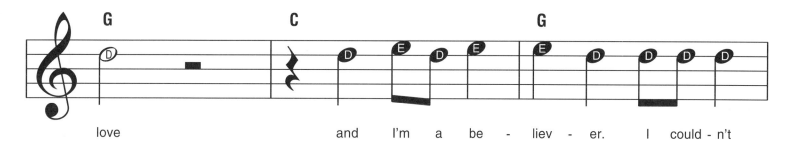

G   C   G

love   and I'm a be - liev - er. I could-n't

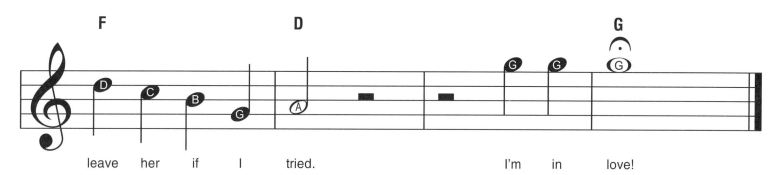

F   D   G

leave her if I tried.   I'm in love!

46

If I Had $1,000,000

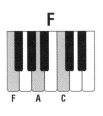
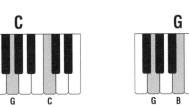
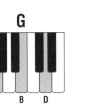
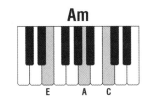

Words and Music by Steven Page
and Ed Robertson

Brightly

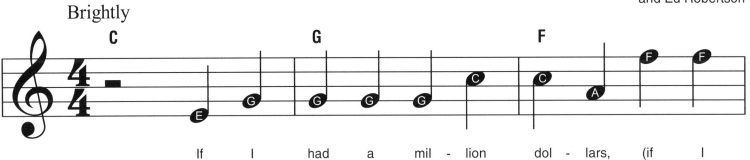

If I had a mil-lion dol-lars, (if I

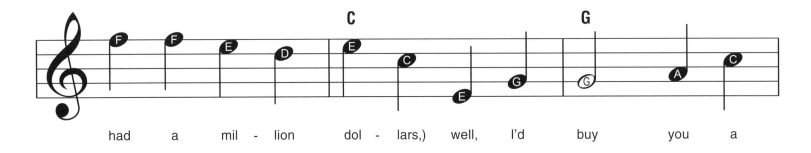

had a mil-lion dol-lars,) well, I'd buy you a

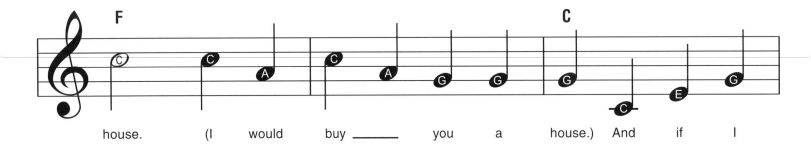

house. (I would buy _____ you a house.) And if I

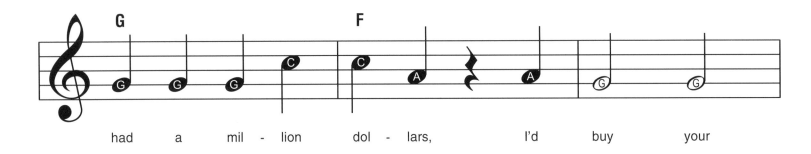

had a mil-lion dol-lars, I'd buy your

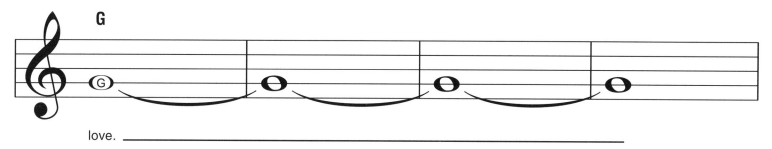

love. _____

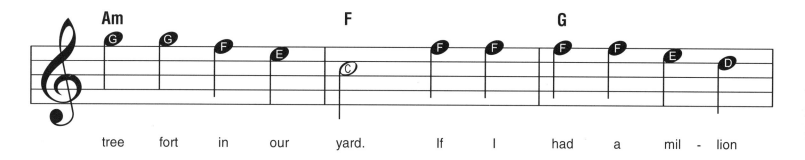

If I had a mil - lion dol - lars, I'd build a

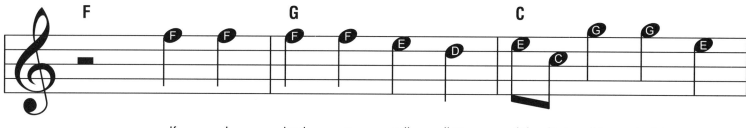

tree fort in our yard. If I had a mil - lion

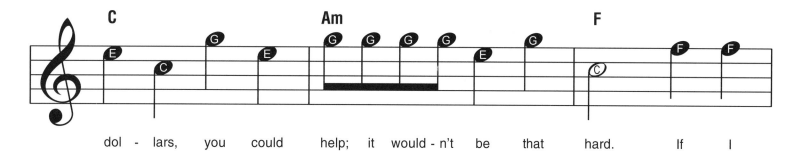

dol - lars, you could help; it would - n't be that hard. If I

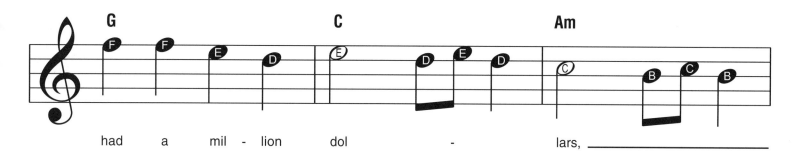

had a mil - lion dol - lars, _____

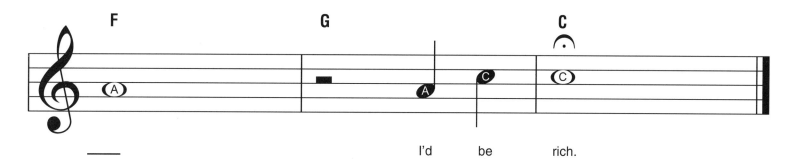

____ I'd be rich.

Iris
from the Motion Picture CITY OF ANGELS

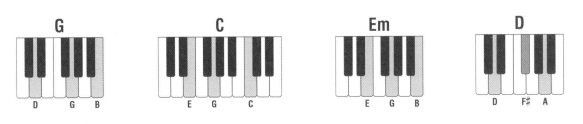

Words and Music by
John Rzeznik

With a steady pulse

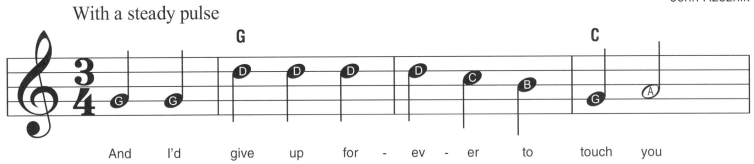

And   I'd   give   up   for - ev - er   to   touch   you

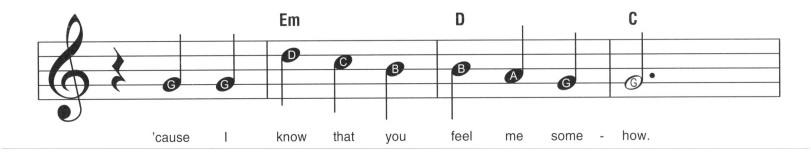

'cause   I   know   that   you   feel   me   some - how.

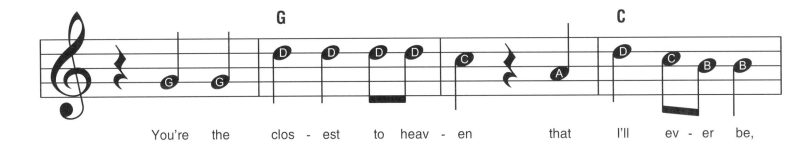

You're   the   clos - est   to   heav - en   that   I'll   ev - er   be,

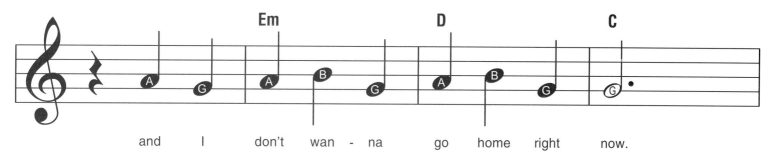

and I don't wan - na go home right now.

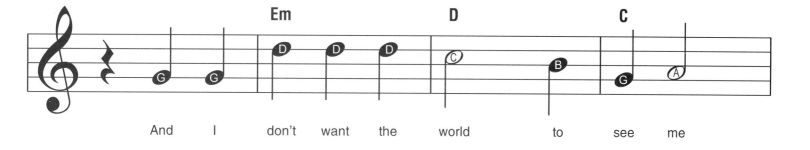

And I don't want the world to see me

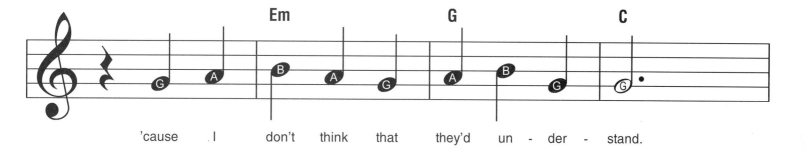

'cause I don't think that they'd un - der - stand.

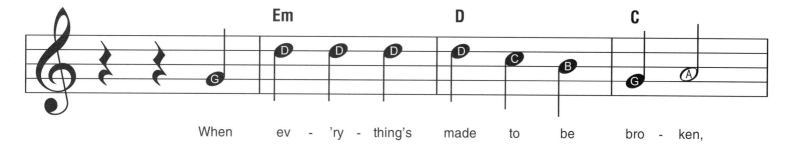

When ev - 'ry - thing's made to be bro - ken,

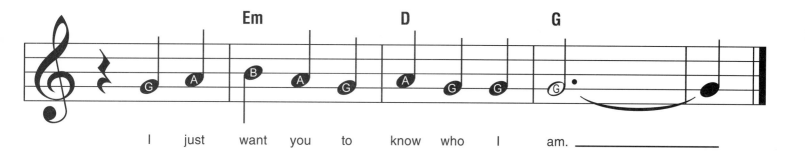

I just want you to know who I am. _____

Jessie's Girl

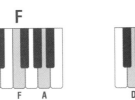
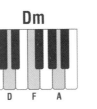
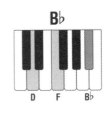
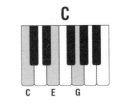

Words and Music by
Rick Springfield

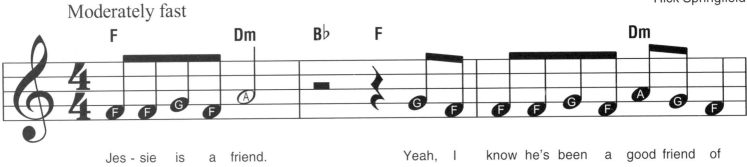

Jes - sie is a friend. Yeah, I know he's been a good friend of

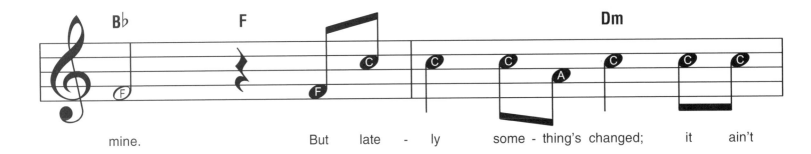

mine. But late - ly some - thing's changed; it ain't

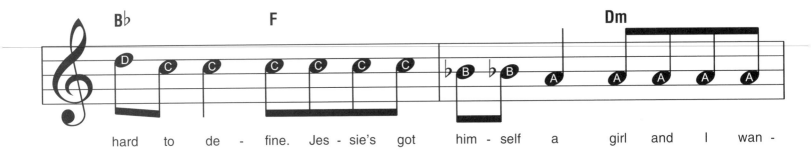

hard to de - fine. Jes - sie's got him - self a girl and I wan -

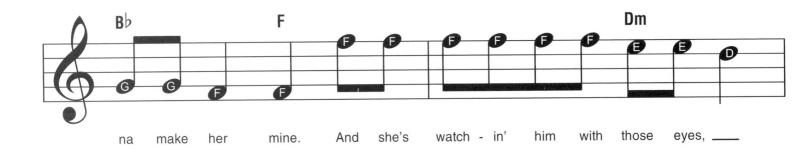

na make her mine. And she's watch - in' him with those eyes, _____

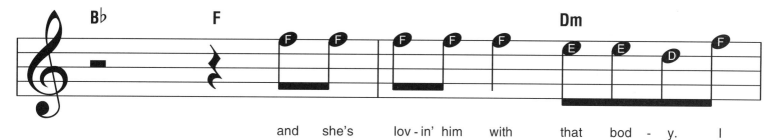

and she's lov-in' him with that bod-y. I

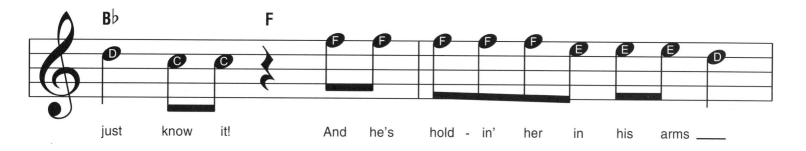

just know it! And he's hold-in' her in his arms ____

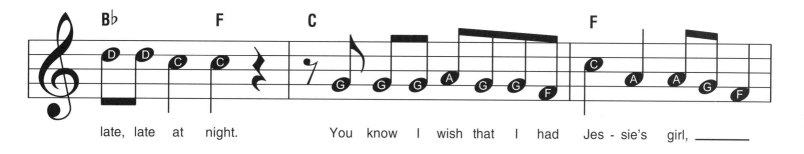

late, late at night. You know I wish that I had Jes-sie's girl, ____

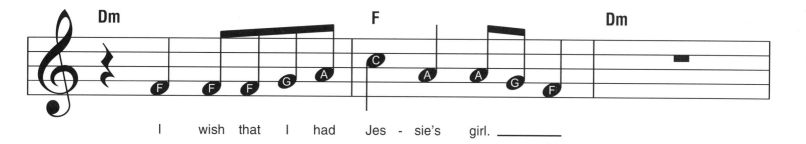

I wish that I had Jes-sie's girl. ____

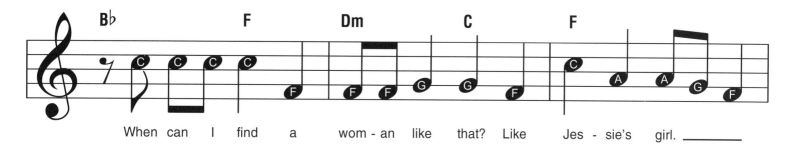

When can I find a wom-an like that? Like Jes-sie's girl. ____

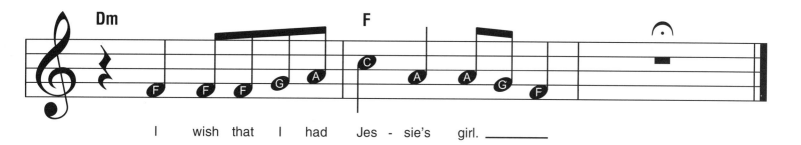

I wish that I had Jes-sie's girl. ____

Knockin' on Heaven's Door

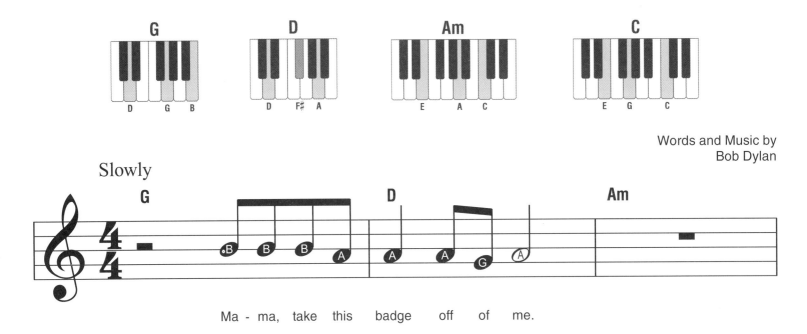

Words and Music by
Bob Dylan

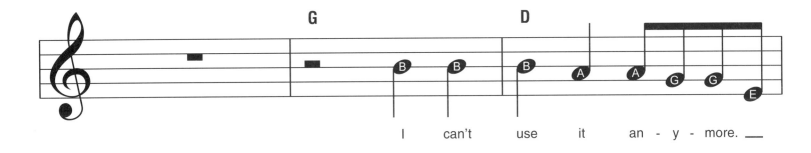

Ma - ma, take this badge off of me.

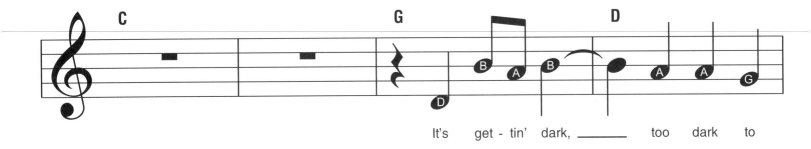

I can't use it an - y - more. ___

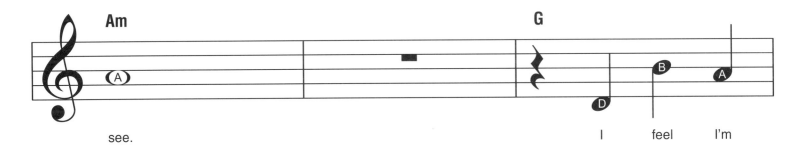

It's get - tin' dark, ___ too dark to

see.   I feel I'm

Last Kiss

Words and Music by
Wayne Cochran

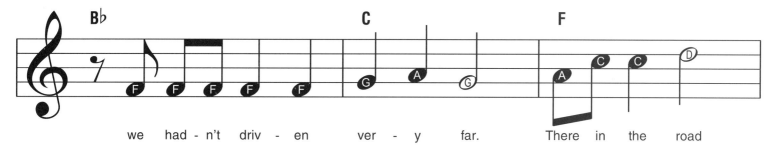

we had - n't driv - en ver - y far. There in the road

straight a - head, a car was stalled; the en - gine was dead.

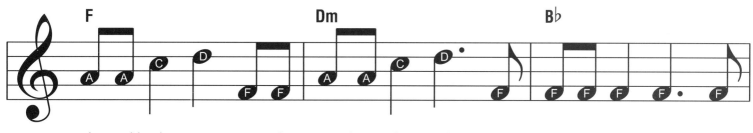

I could - n't stop, so I swerved to the right. I'll nev - er for - get the

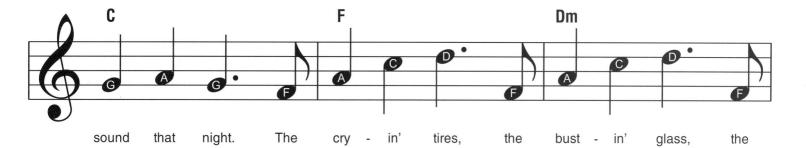

sound that night. The cry - in' tires, the bust - in' glass, the

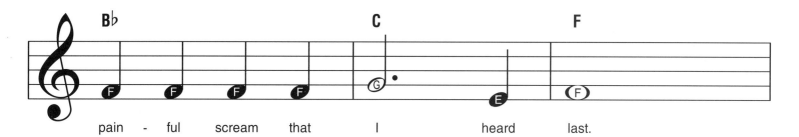

pain - ful scream that I heard last.

D.S. al Coda
(Return to 𝄋, play to ⊕
and skip to Coda)

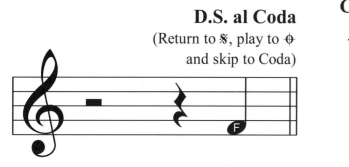

Well,

CODA

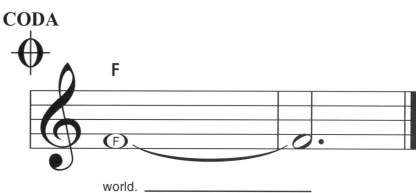

world. _____

Learning to Fly

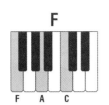 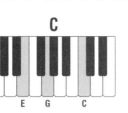 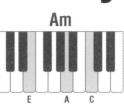 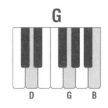

F   C   Am   G

Words and Music by Tom Petty
and Jeff Lynne

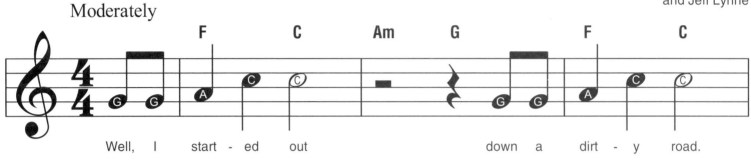

Well, I start - ed out   down a dirt - y road.

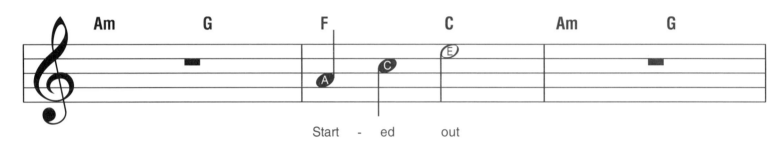

Start - ed out

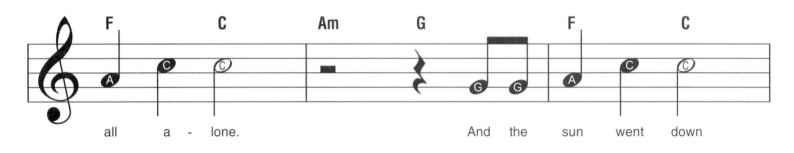

all a - lone.   And the sun went down

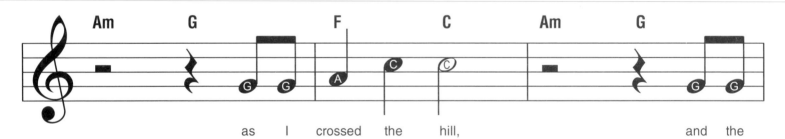

as I crossed the hill,   and the

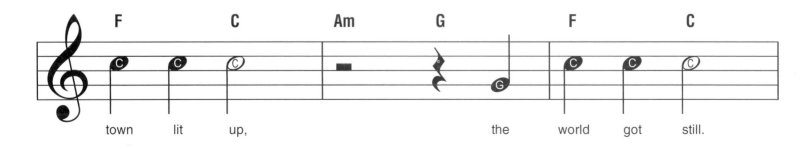

town lit up,   the world got still.

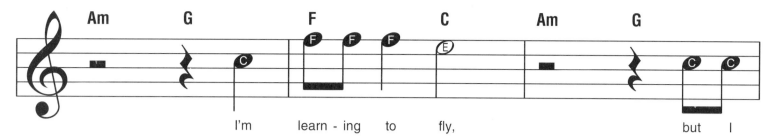

I'm learn - ing to fly, but I

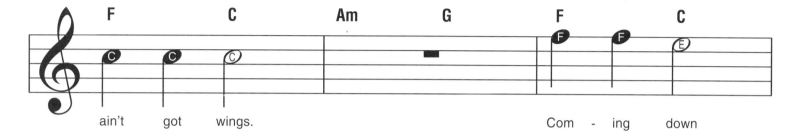

ain't got wings. Com - ing down

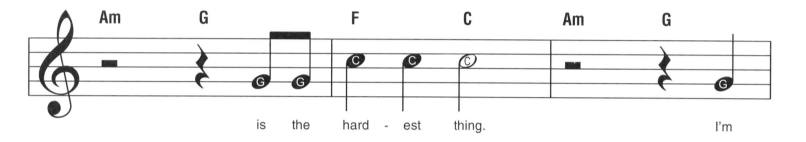

is the hard - est thing. I'm

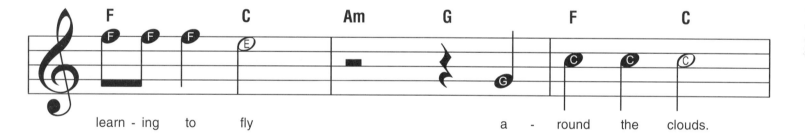

learn - ing to fly a - round the clouds.

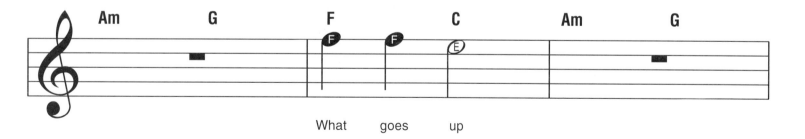

What goes up

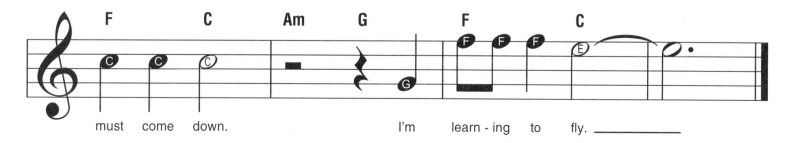

must come down. I'm learn - ing to fly. _____

Let Her Cry

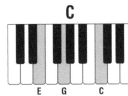
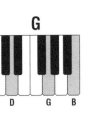
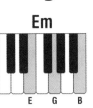
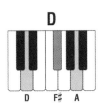

Words and Music by Darius Rucker,
Dean Felber, Mark Bryan
and Jim Sonefeld

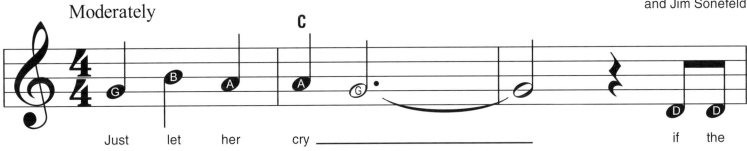

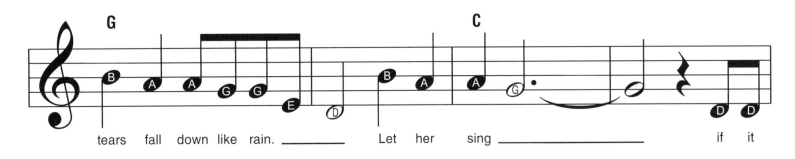

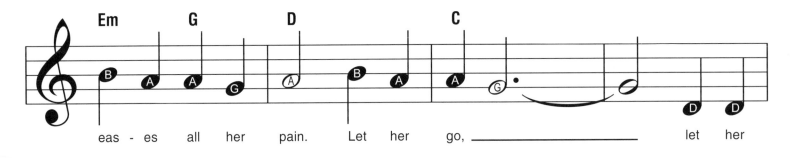

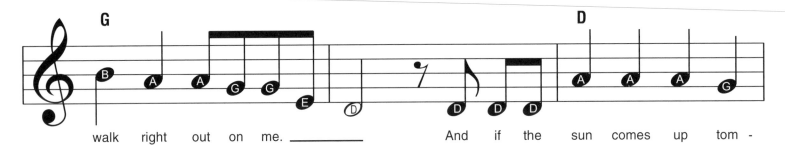

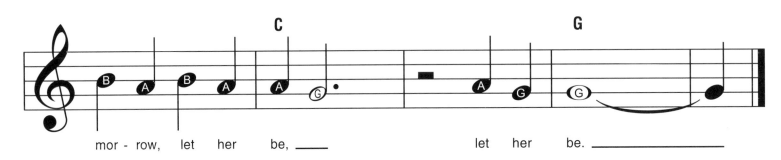

Let the Sunshine In
from the Broadway Musical Production HAIR

Let It Be

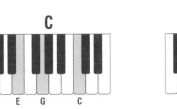
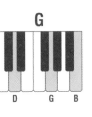
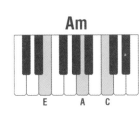
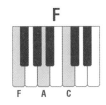

Words and Music by John Lennon
and Paul McCartney

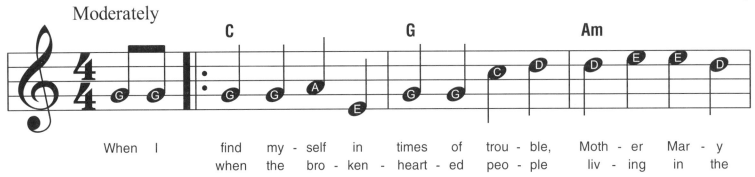

When I find my - self in times of trou - ble, Moth - er Mar - y
when the bro - ken - heart - ed peo - ple liv - ing in the

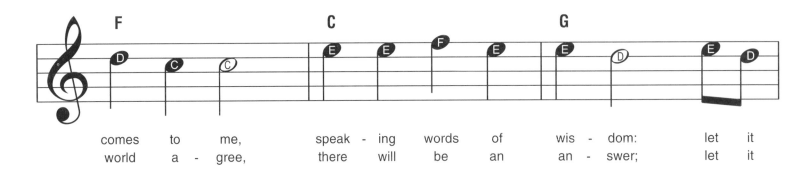

comes to me, speak - ing words of wis - dom: let it
world a - gree, there will be an an - swer; let it

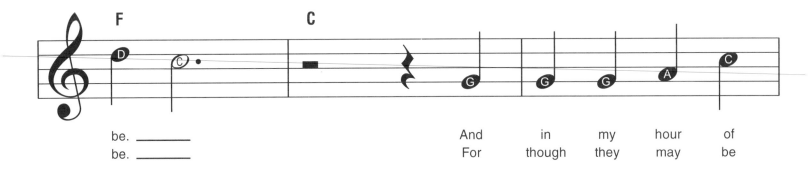

be. _____ And in my hour of
be. _____ For though they may be

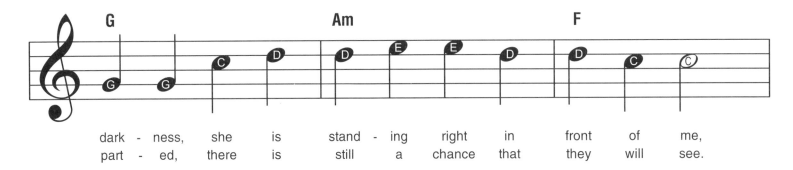

dark - ness, she is stand - ing right in front of me,
part - ed, there is still a chance that they will see.

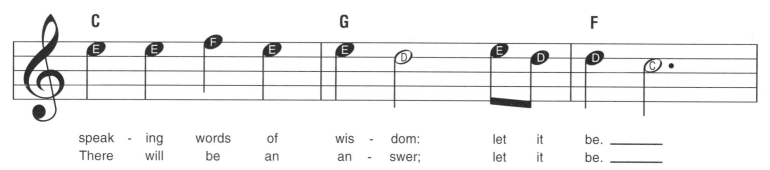

speak - ing words of wis - dom: let it be. _____
There will be an an - swer; let it be. _____

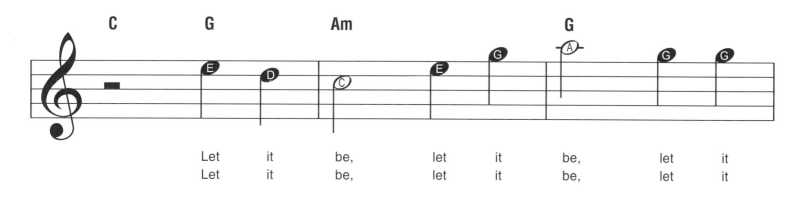

Let it be, let it be, let it
Let it be, let it be, let it

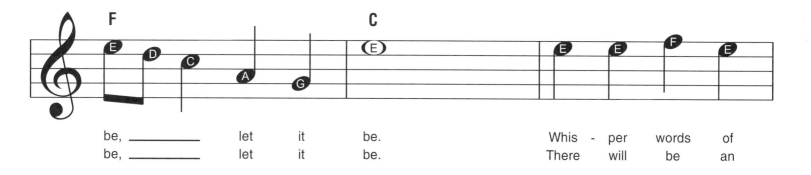

be, _____ let it be. Whis - per words of
be, _____ let it be. There will be an

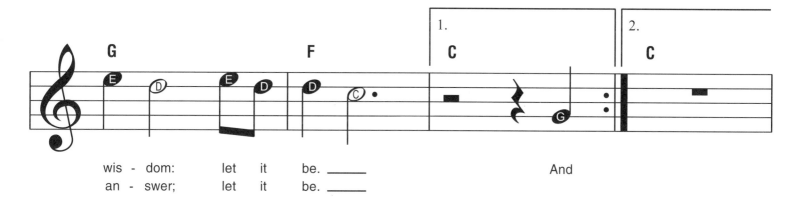

wis - dom: let it be. _____ And
an - swer; let it be. _____

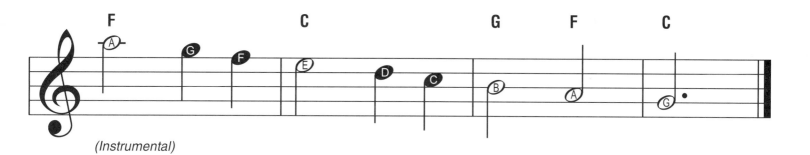

(Instrumental)

61

Massachusetts
(The Lights Went Out)

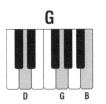 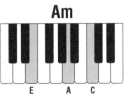 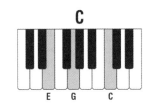 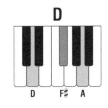

Words and Music by Barry Gibb,
Robin Gibb and Maurice Gibb

Moderately

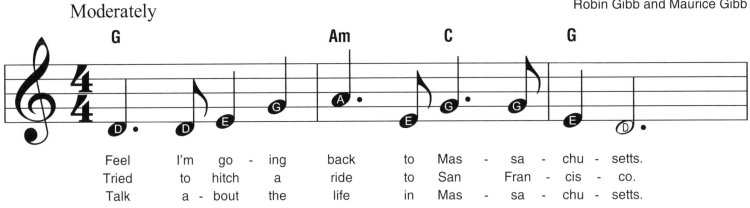

Feel I'm go - ing back to Mas - sa - chu - setts.
Tried to hitch a ride to San Fran - cis - co.
Talk a - bout the life in Mas - sa - chu - setts.

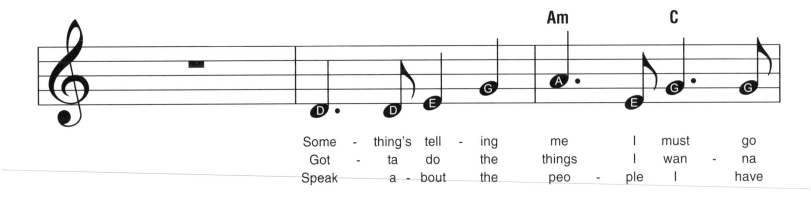

Some - thing's tell - ing me I must go
Got - ta do the things I wan - na
Speak a - bout the peo - ple I have

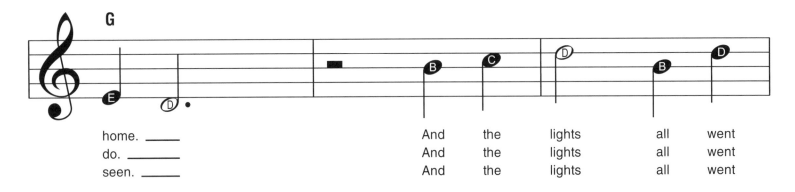

home. _____ And the lights all went
do. _____ And the lights all went
seen. _____ And the lights all went

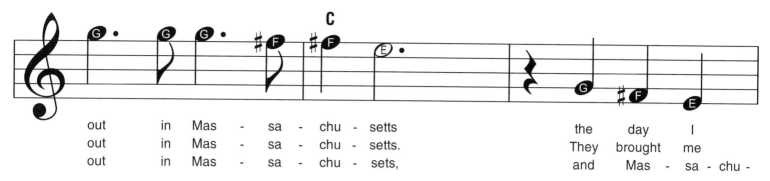

out in Mas - sa - chu - setts   the day I
out in Mas - sa - chu - setts.   They brought me
out in Mas - sa - chu - sets,   and Mas - sa - chu -

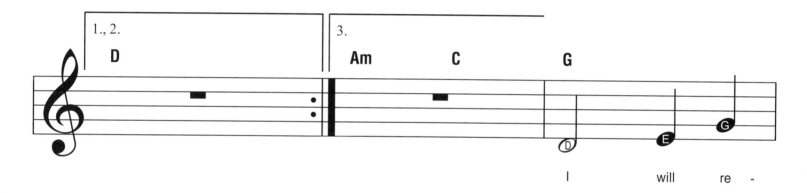

left   her   stand - ing   on   her   own.
back   to   see   my   way   with   you.
setts   is   one   place   I   have   seen.

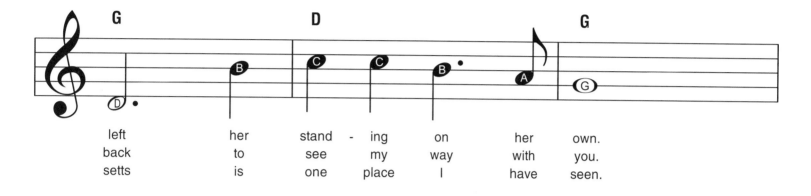

I   will   re -

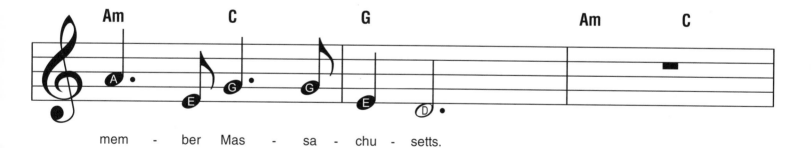

mem - ber Mas - sa - chu - setts.

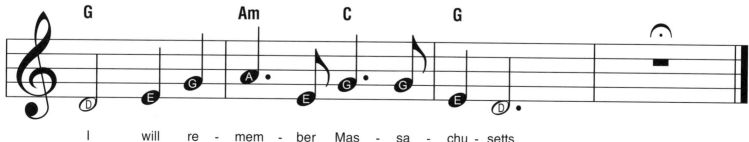

I   will   re - mem - ber Mas - sa - chu - setts.

No Rain

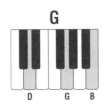
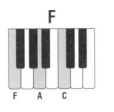
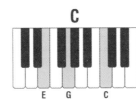
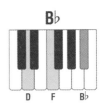

Words and Music by
Blind Melon

Moderately fast

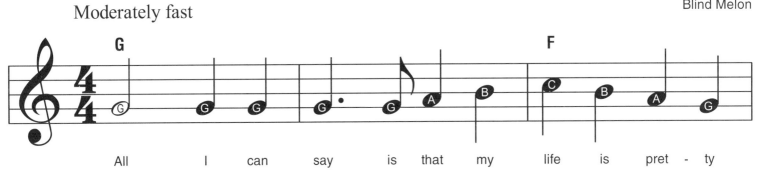

All I can say is that my life is pret - ty

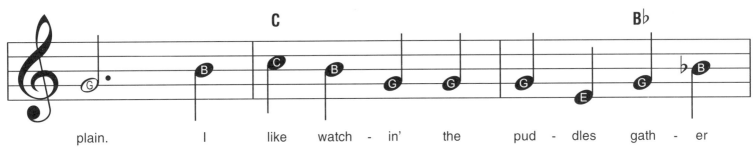

plain. I like watch - in' the pud - dles gath - er

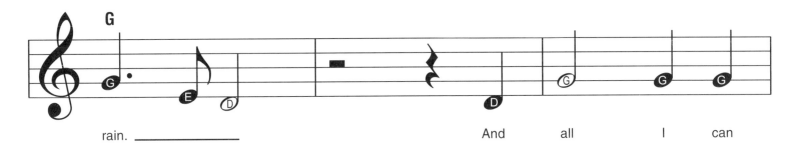

rain. _____ And all I can

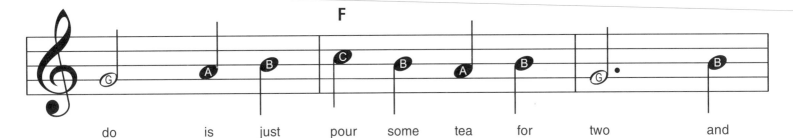

do is just pour some tea for two and

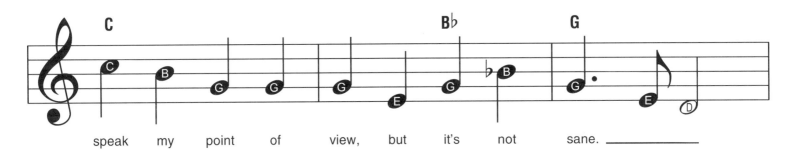

speak my point of view, but it's not sane. _____

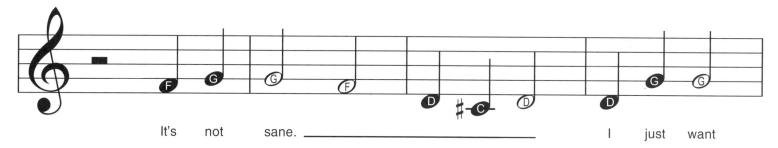

It's not sane. _____ I just want

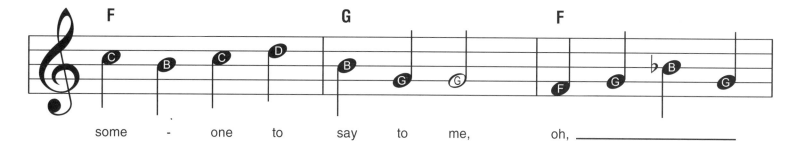

some - one to say to me, oh, _____

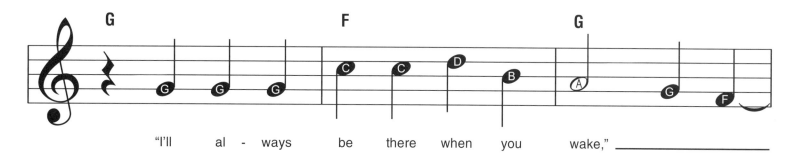

"I'll al - ways be there when you wake," _____

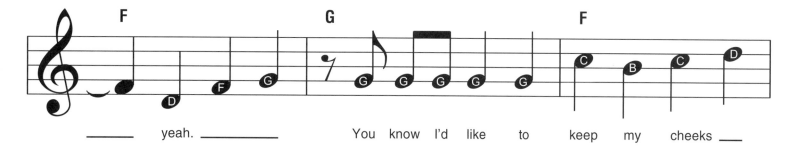

_____ yeah. _____ You know I'd like to keep my cheeks ___

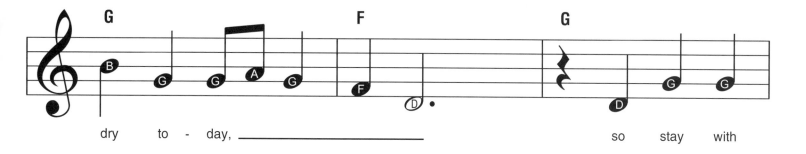

dry to - day, _____ so stay with

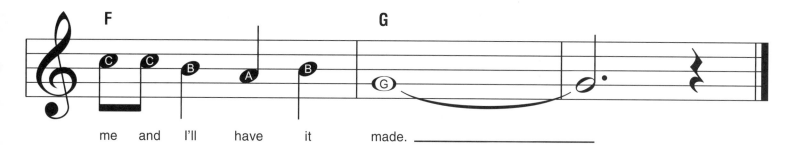

me and I'll have it made. _____

No Woman No Cry

Words and Music by
Vincent Ford

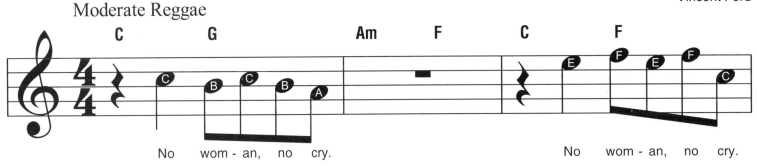

No wom-an, no cry. No wom-an, no cry.

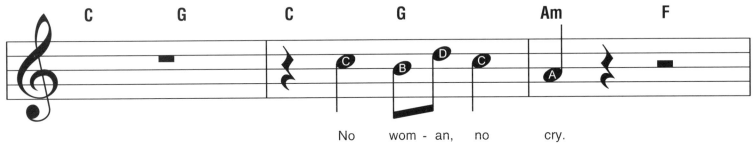

No wom-an, no cry.

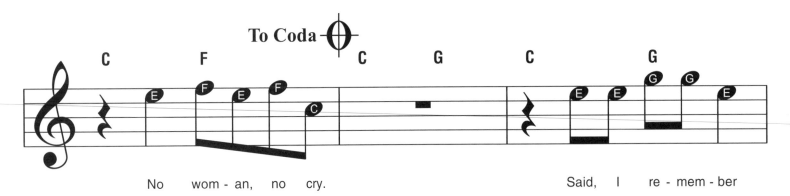

No wom-an, no cry. Said, I re-mem-ber

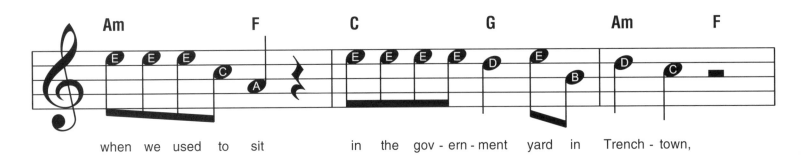

when we used to sit in the gov-ern-ment yard in Trench-town,

ob - a - ob - a - serv - ing the hyp - o - crites as they would

min - gle with the good peo - ple we meet,

good friends we had, oh, good friends we've lost a - long the

way. In this bright fu - ture, you can't for - get your past,

D.C. al Coda
(Return to beginning,
play to ⊕ and skip to Coda)

CODA

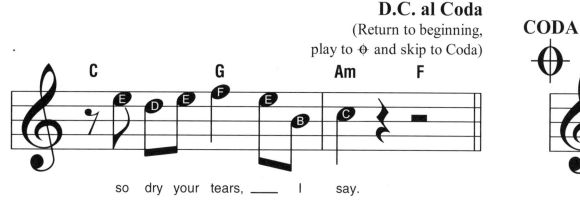

so dry your tears, ___ I say.

One of Us

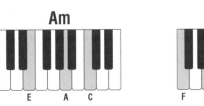
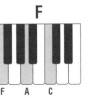
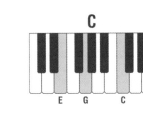
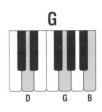

Words and Music by
Eric Bazilian

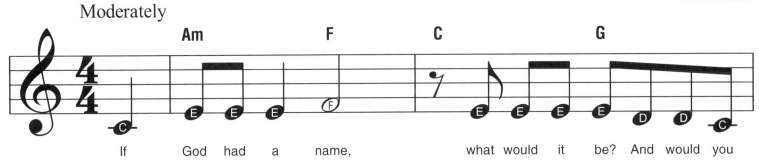

If God had a name, what would it be? And would you

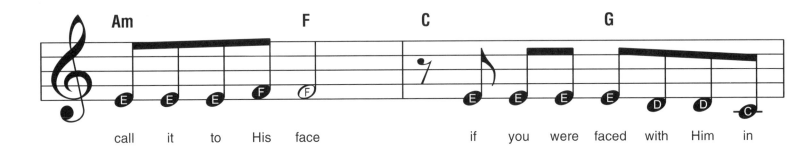

call it to His face if you were faced with Him in

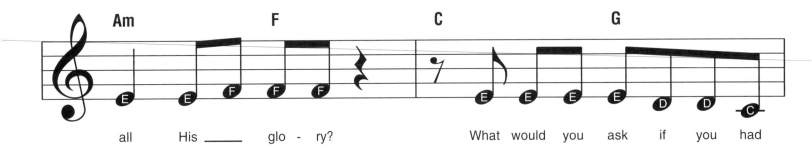

all His ____ glo - ry? What would you ask if you had

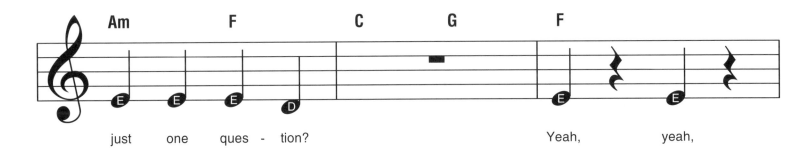

just one ques - tion? Yeah, yeah,

God is ___ great. Yeah, yeah, God is ___ good.

Yeah, yeah, yeah, yeah, yeah. What if God was one of us,

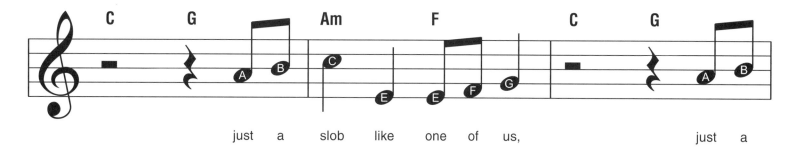

just a slob like one of us, just a

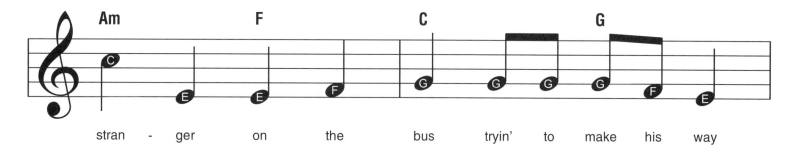

stran - ger on the bus tryin' to make his way

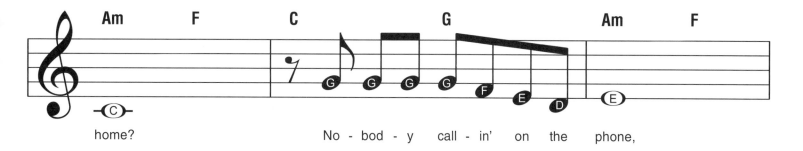

home? No - bod - y call - in' on the phone,

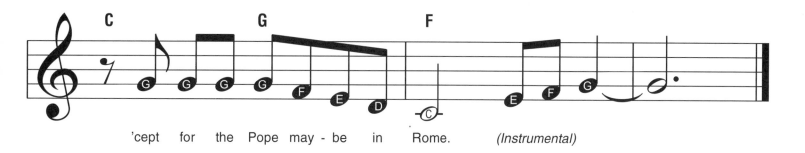

'cept for the Pope may - be in Rome. *(Instrumental)*

Peaceful Easy Feeling

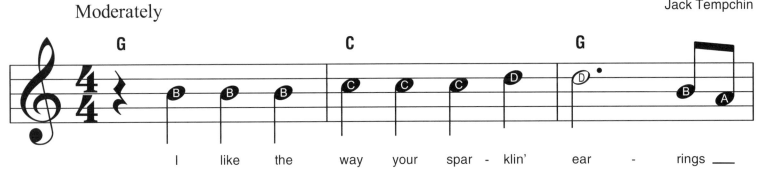

Words and Music by
Jack Tempchin

Moderately

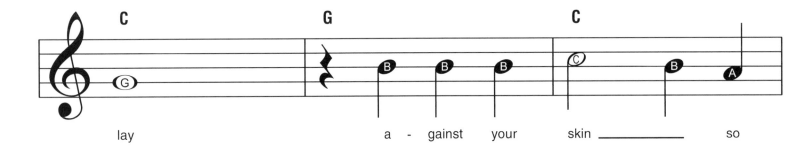

I like the way your spar-klin' ear - rings ___

lay   a - gainst your   skin _____ so

brown.   And   I   wan - na

sleep   with   you   in   the   des - ert _____ to - night

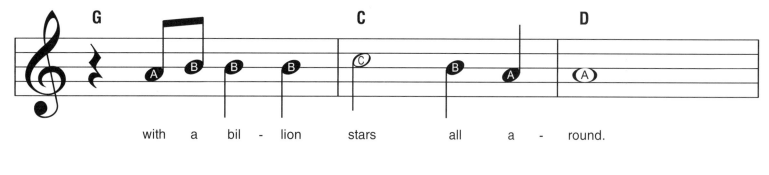

with a bil - lion stars all a - round.

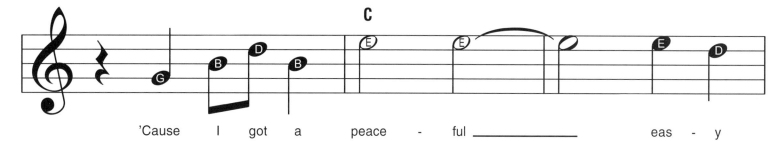

'Cause I got a peace - ful _____ eas - y

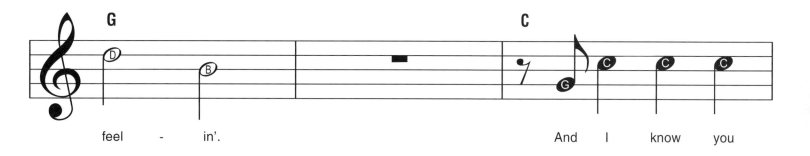

feel - in'. And I know you

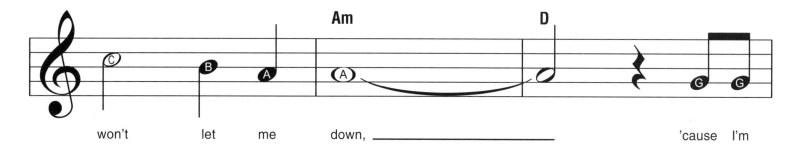

won't let me down, _____ 'cause I'm

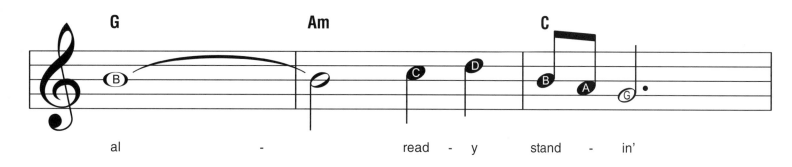

al - read - y stand - in'

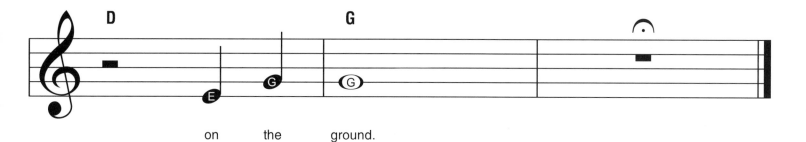

on the ground.

Pink Houses

Words and Music by
John Mellencamp

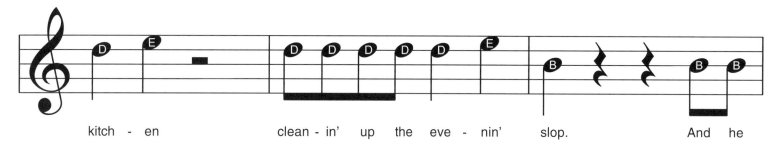

kitch - en   clean - in' up the eve - nin' slop.   And he

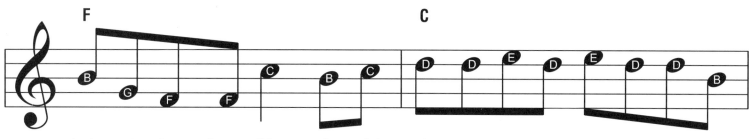

looks   at   her and says, "Hey,   dar - lin',   I can re - mem - ber when you   could ___

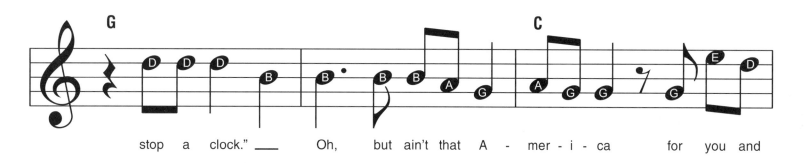

stop   a   clock." ___   Oh,   but   ain't that   A - mer - i - ca   for   you and

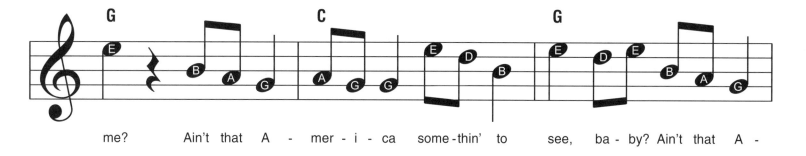

me?   Ain't that   A - mer - i - ca   some - thin' to   see,   ba - by? Ain't that   A -

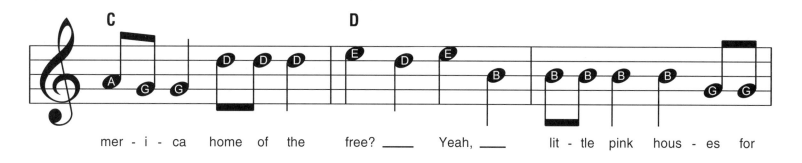

mer - i - ca   home of   the   free? ___   Yeah, ___   lit - tle pink   hous - es   for

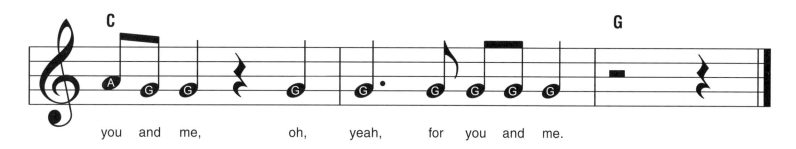

you and   me,   oh,   yeah,   for   you and   me.

Poker Face

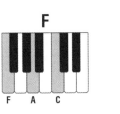
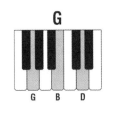
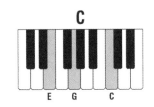

Words and Music by Stefani Germanotta
and RedOne

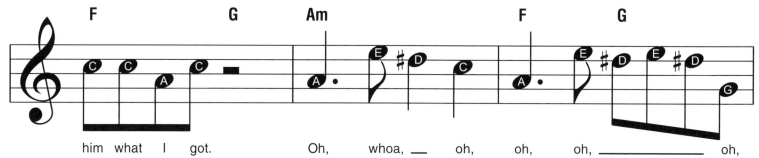

him what I got.   Oh,   whoa, — oh,   oh,   oh, ——————————— oh,

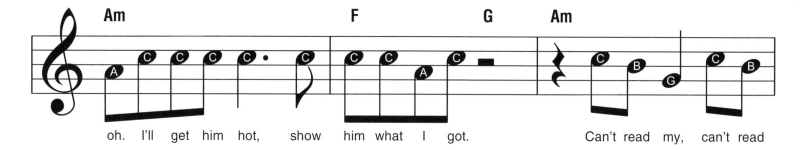

oh. I'll get him hot,   show   him what I got.   Can't read my,   can't read

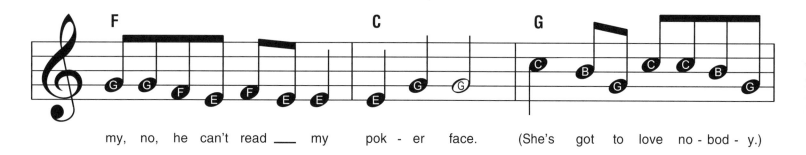

my, no, he can't read __ my   pok - er face.   (She's got to love no - bod - y.)

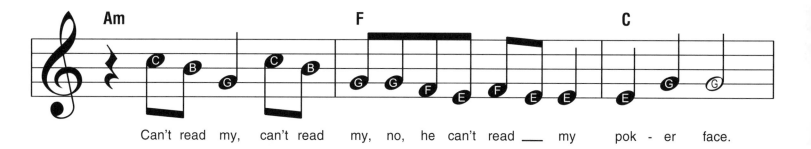

Can't read my,   can't read   my, no, he can't read __ my   pok - er face.

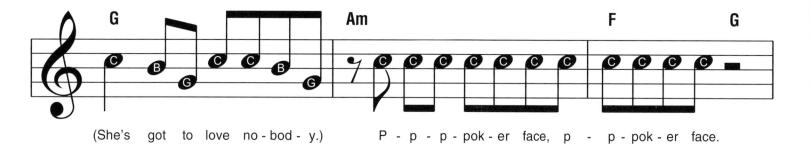

(She's got to love no - bod - y.)   P - p - p - pok - er face, p - p - pok - er face.

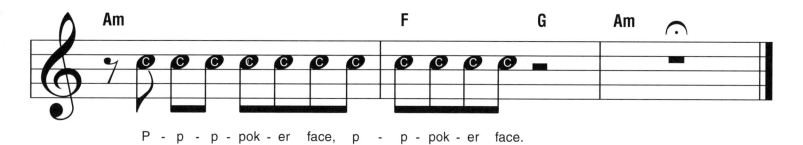

P - p - p - pok - er face, p - p - pok - er face.

Roar

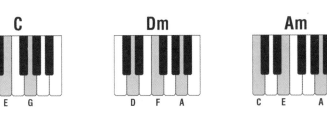

Words and Music by Katy Perry,
Max Martin, Dr. Luke,
Bonnie McKee and Henry Walter

Run-Around

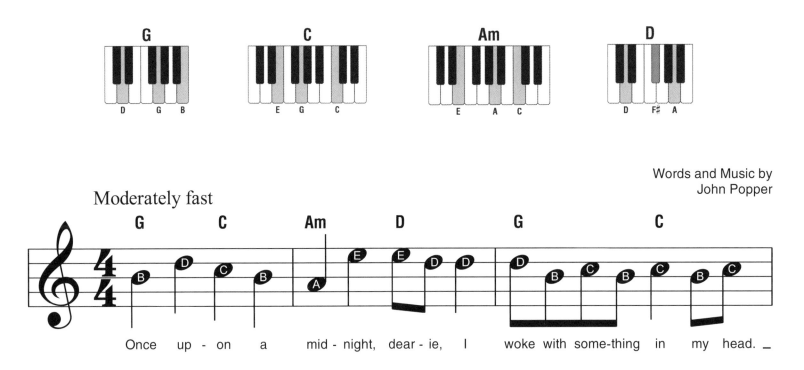

Words and Music by
John Popper

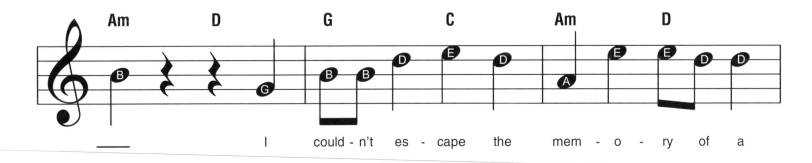

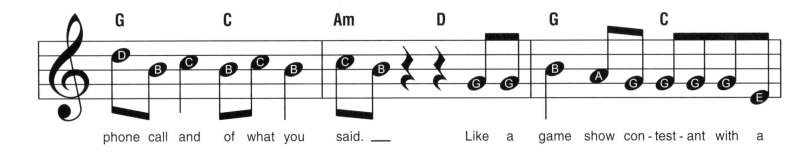

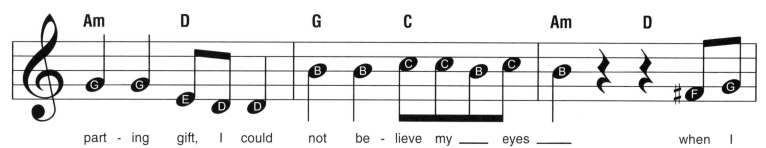

part - ing gift, I could not be - lieve my ___ eyes ___ when I

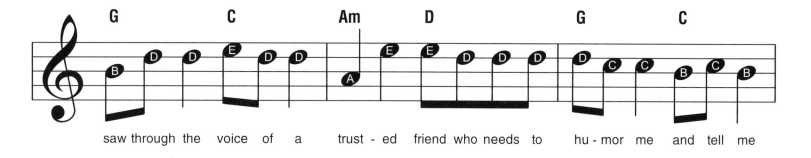

saw through the voice of a trust - ed friend who needs to hu - mor me and tell me

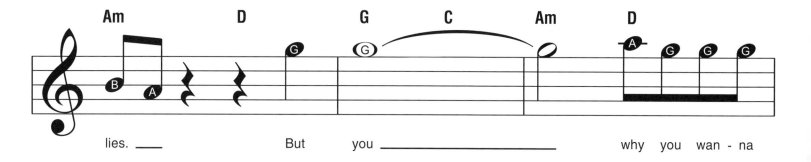

lies. ___ But you _____ why you wan - na

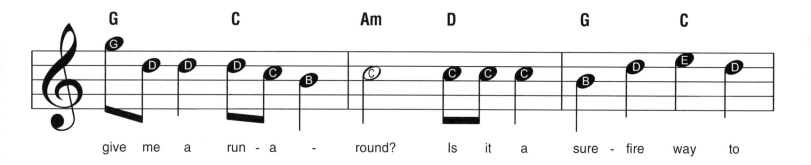

give me a run - a - round? Is it a sure - fire way to

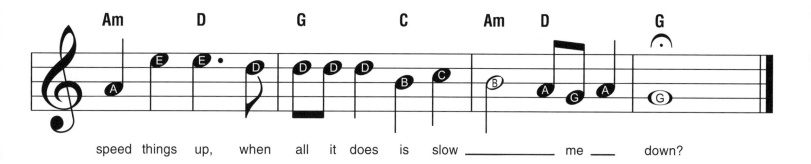

speed things up, when all it does is slow _____ me ___ down?

Save Tonight

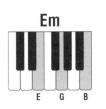
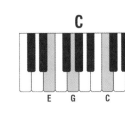
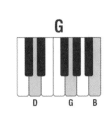
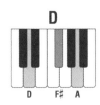

Words and Music by
Eagle Eye Cherry

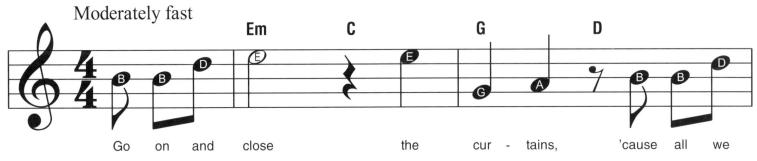

Go on and close the cur - tains, 'cause all we

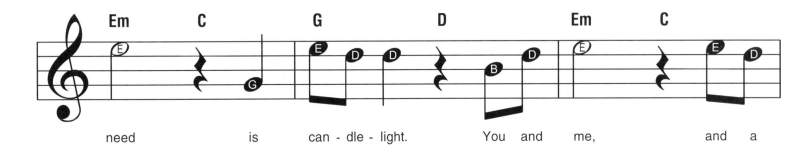

need is can - dle - light. You and me, and a

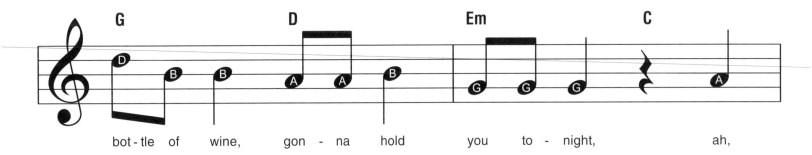

bot - tle of wine, gon - na hold you to - night, ah,

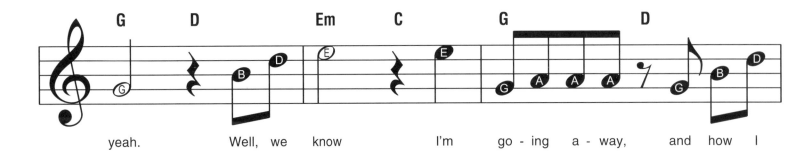

yeah. Well, we know I'm go - ing a - way, and how I

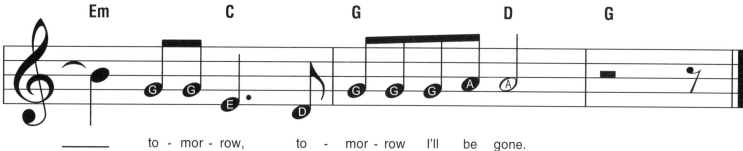

The Scientist

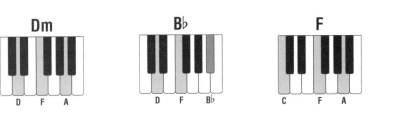

Words and Music by Guy Berryman,
Jon Buckland, Will Champion
and Chris Martin

Moderately slow

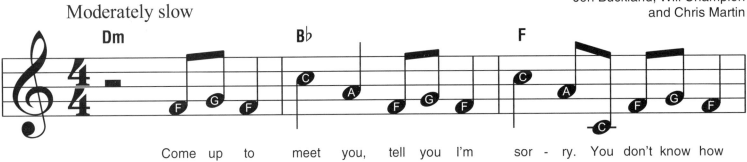

Come up to meet you, tell you I'm sor - ry. You don't know how

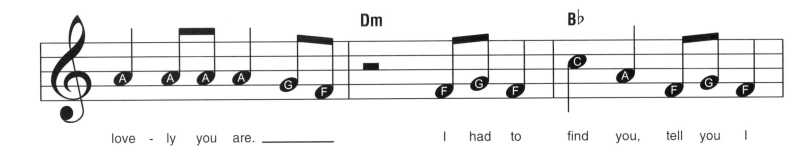

love - ly you are. _____ I had to find you, tell you I

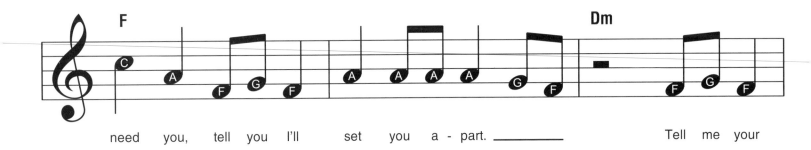

need you, tell you I'll set you a - part. _____ Tell me your

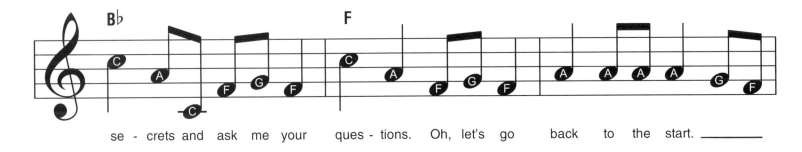

se - crets and ask me your ques - tions. Oh, let's go back to the start. _____

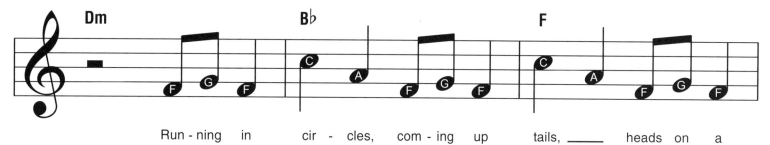

Run - ning in cir - cles, com - ing up tails, _____ heads on a

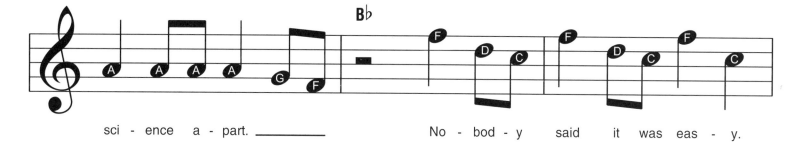

sci - ence a - part. _____ No - bod - y said it was eas - y.

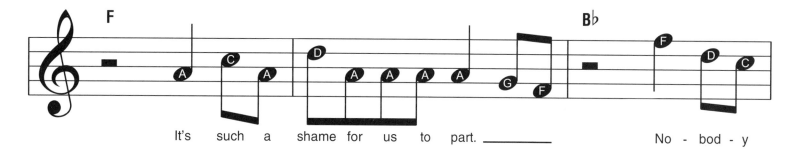

It's such a shame for us to part. _____ No - bod - y

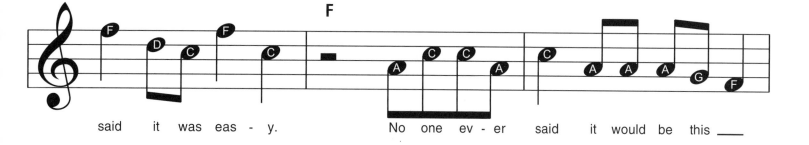

said it was eas - y. No one ev - er said it would be this _____

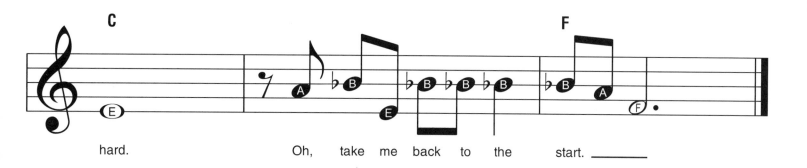

hard. Oh, take me back to the start. _____

7 Years

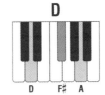

Words and Music by Lukas Forchhammer,
Morten Ristorp, Stefan Forrest,
David Labrel, Christopher Brown
and Morten Pilegaard

world, but   we thought we   were   big - ger.   Push - ing each oth - er   to   the
dream __ like   my dad - dy be - fore   me,   so   I   start - ed   writ - ing

lim - its,   we   were learn - ing quick - er.   By   e - lev - en, smok - ing
songs,   I   start - ed   writ - ing   sto - ries.   Some - thing a - bout that glo - ry

herb   and drink - ing burn - ing   li - quor.   Nev - er   rich, so   we   were
just   al - ways seemed   to   bore   me,   'cause on - ly those   I   real - ly

1.

out   to   make that stead - y   fig - ure.

2.

D.C. al Coda
(Return to beginning, play
D to ⊕ and skip to Coda)

love   will   ev - er   real - ly know me.

CODA

Once   I   was sev - en years   old.

Some Nights

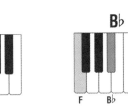
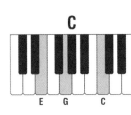
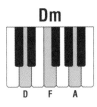

Words and Music by Jeff Bhasker,
Andrew Dost, Jack Antonoff
and Nate Ruess

Moderately

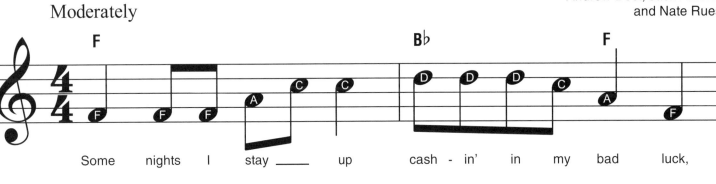

Some nights I stay ___ up cash - in' in my bad luck,

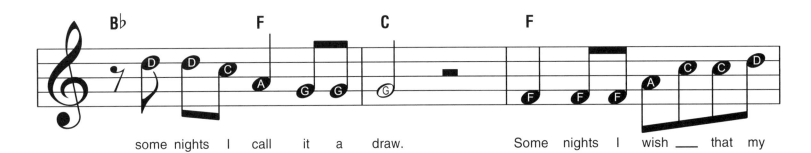

some nights I call it a draw. Some nights I wish ___ that my

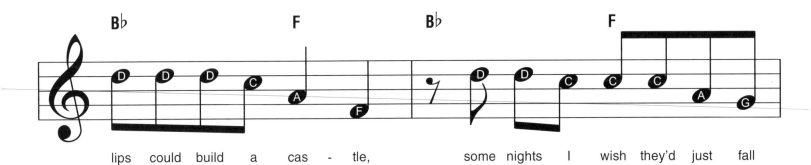

lips could build a cas - tle, some nights I wish they'd just fall

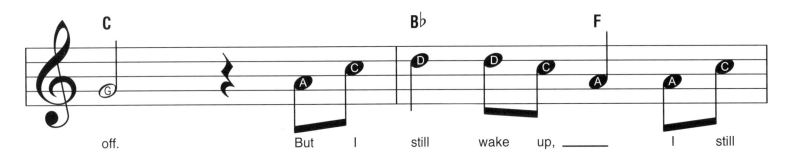

off. But I still wake up, ___ I still

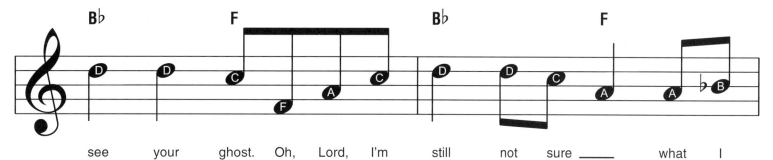

see your ghost. Oh, Lord, I'm still not sure _____ what I

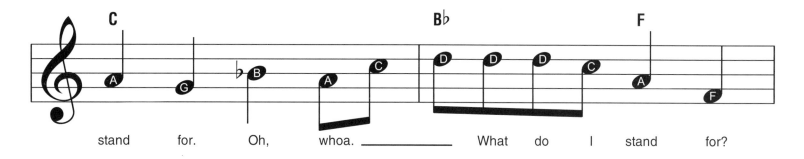

stand for. Oh, whoa. _____ What do I stand for?

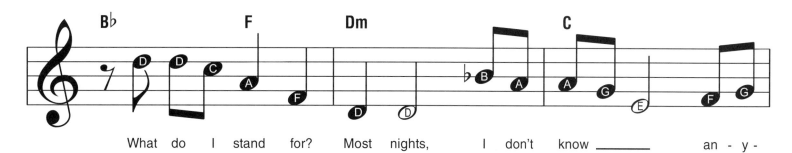

What do I stand for? Most nights, I don't know _____ an - y -

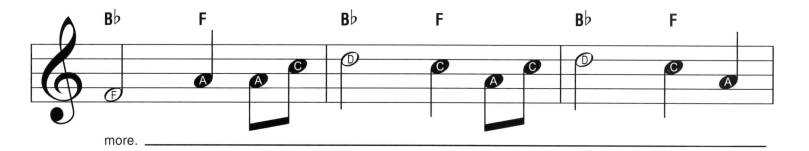

more. _____

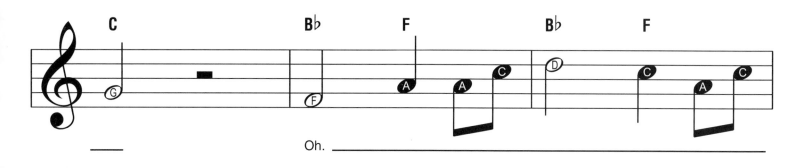

_____ Oh. _____

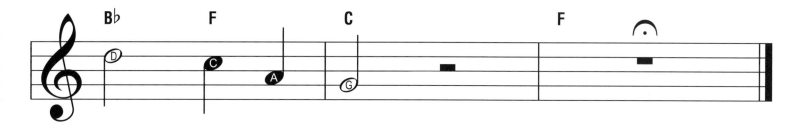

Southern Cross

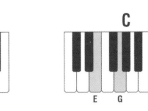
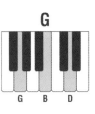

Words and Music by Stephen Stills,
Richard Curtis and Michael Curtis

Moderately fast

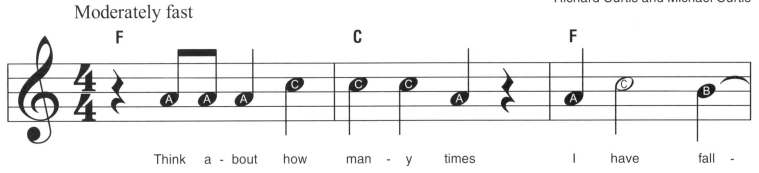

Think a - bout how man - y times   I have fall -

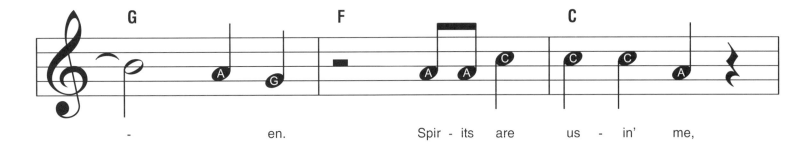

- en.   Spir - its are us - in' me,

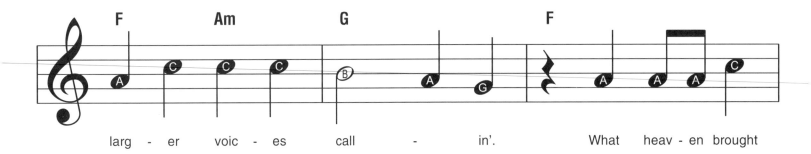

larg - er voic - es call - in'.   What heav - en brought

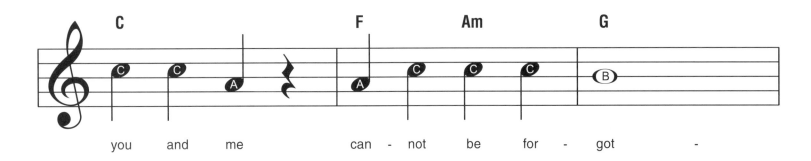

you and me   can - not be for - got -

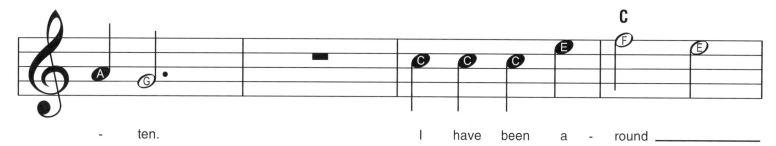

- ten. I have been a - round _____

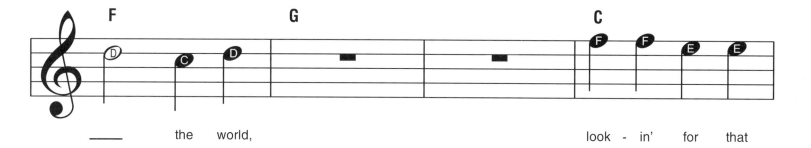

_____ the world, look - in' for that

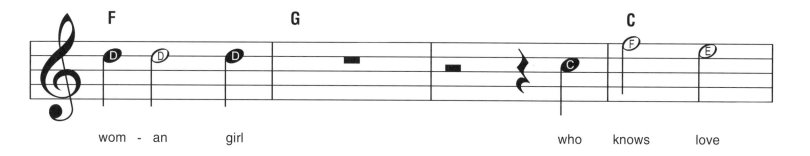

wom - an girl who knows love

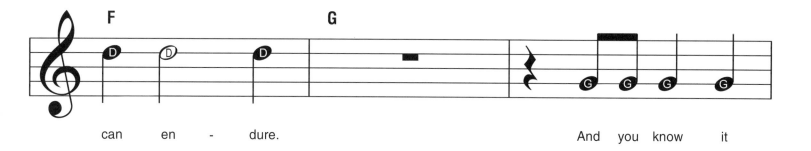

can en - dure. And you know it

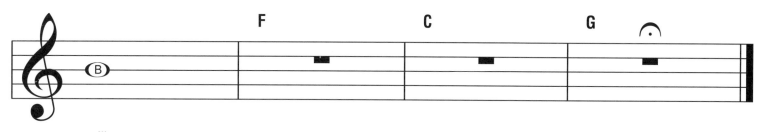

will.

Stand by Me

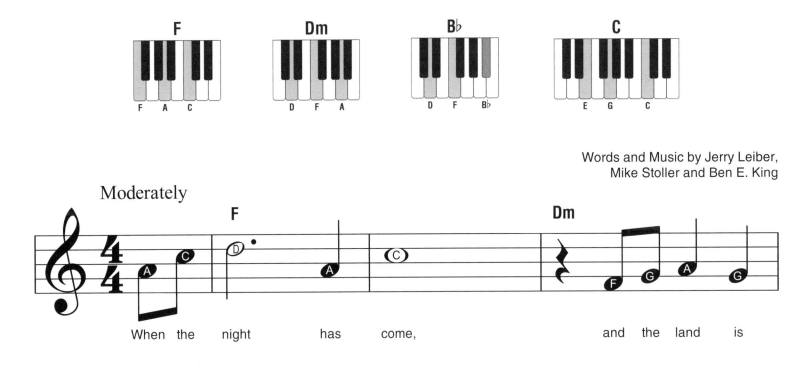

Words and Music by Jerry Leiber,
Mike Stoller and Ben E. King

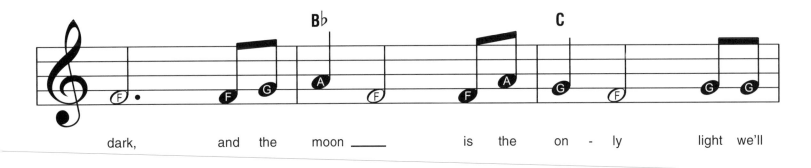

Suzanne

Words and Music by
Leonard Cohen

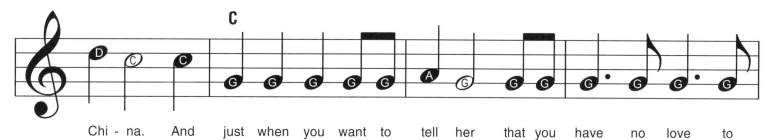

Chi - na. And just when you want to tell her that you have no love to

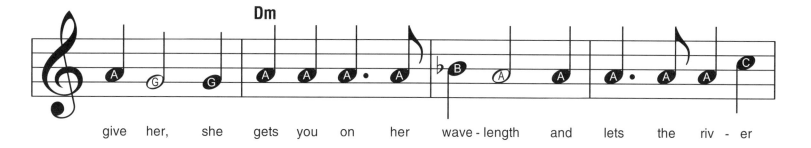

give her, she gets you on her wave - length and lets the riv - er

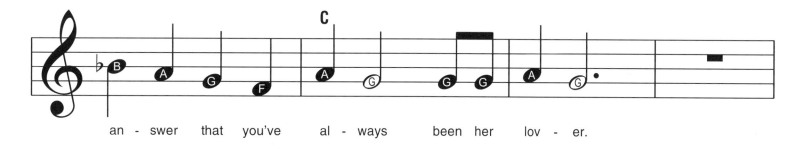

an - swer that you've al - ways been her lov - er.

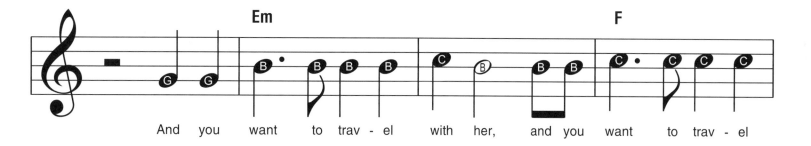

And you want to trav - el with her, and you want to trav - el

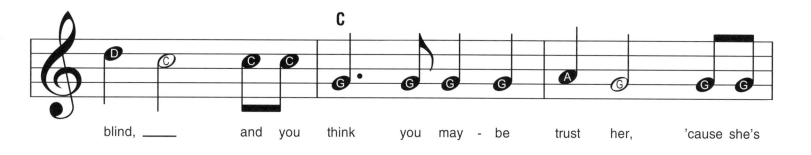

blind, _____ and you think you may - be trust her, 'cause she's

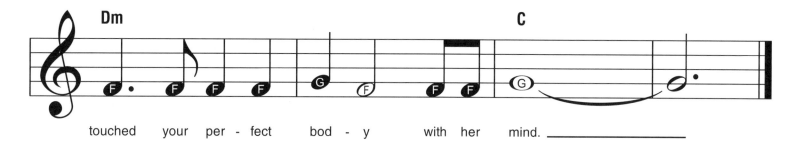

touched your per - fect bod - y with her mind. _____

Teardrops on My Guitar

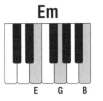
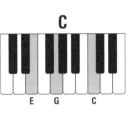
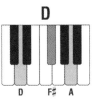

Words and Music by Taylor Swift
and Liz Rose

Moderately fast

Drew looks at me. I
Drew talks to me. I

fake a smile so he won't see that I _____
laugh 'cause it's so damn fun - ny that I _____

want and I'm _____ need - in' ev - 'ry - thing that we should
can't e - ven see an - y - one when he's with

be. I'll bet she's beau - ti - ful, that girl he talks a - bout.
me. He says he's so in love, he's fi - n'lly got it right.

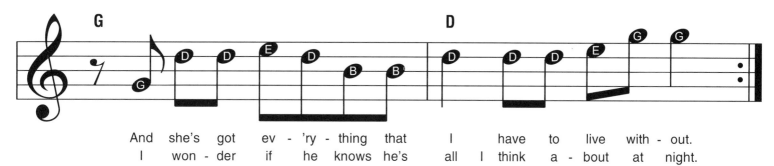

And she's got ev - 'ry - thing that I have to live with - out.
I won - der if he knows he's all I think a - bout at night.

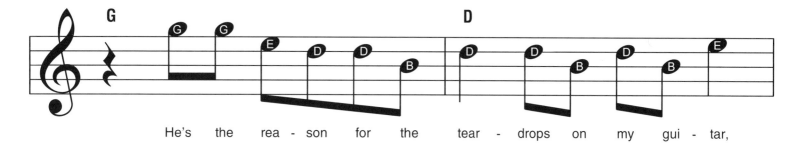

He's the rea - son for the tear - drops on my gui - tar,

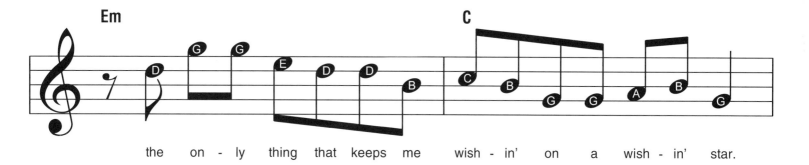

the on - ly thing that keeps me wish - in' on a wish - in' star.

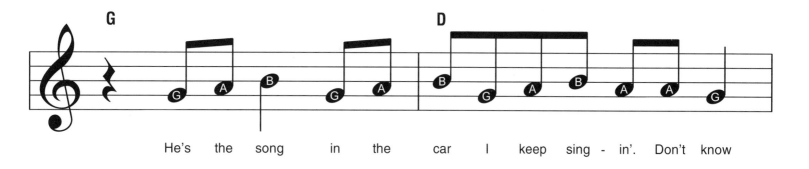

He's the song in the car I keep sing - in'. Don't know

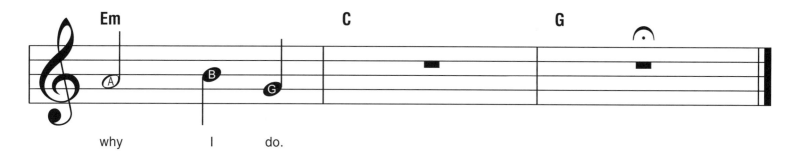

why I do.

That'll Be the Day

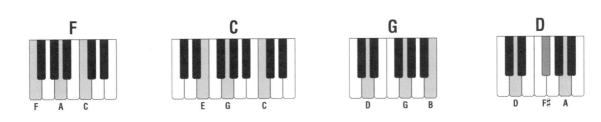

Words and Music by Jerry Allison,
Norman Petty and Buddy Holly

Moderately fast Shuffle

Well, ___ that - 'll be the day, when you say good - bye. Yes, ___

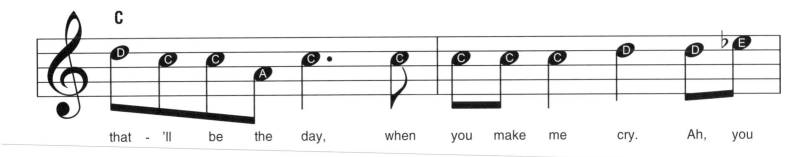

that - 'll be the day, when you make me cry. Ah, you

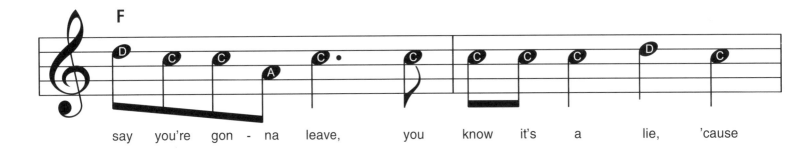

say you're gon - na leave, you know it's a lie, 'cause

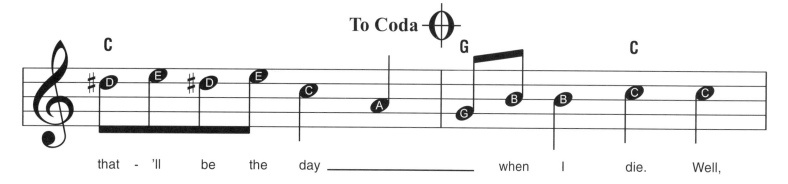

To Coda ⊕

that - 'll be the day _____ when I die. Well,

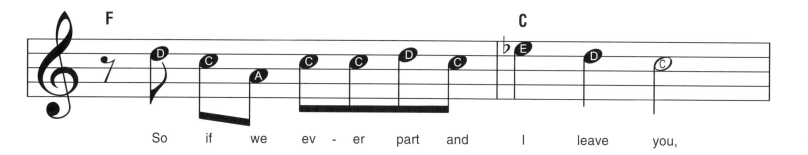

when Cu - pid shot his dart, he shot it at your heart.

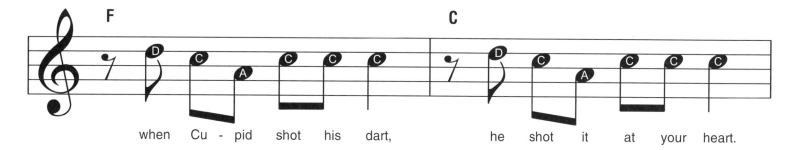

So if we ev - er part and I leave you,

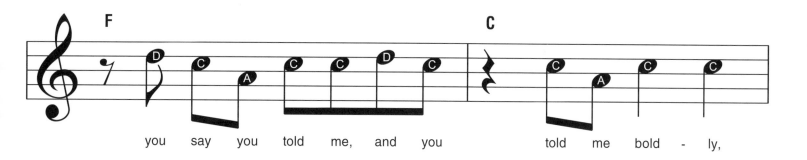

you say you told me, and you told me bold - ly,

D.S. al Coda
(Return to 𝄋, play to ⊕
and skip to Coda)

CODA
⊕

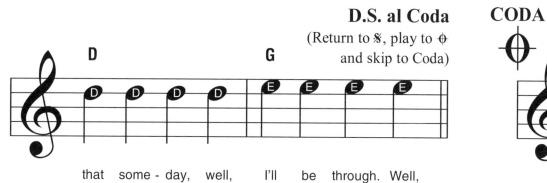

that some - day, well, I'll be through. Well,

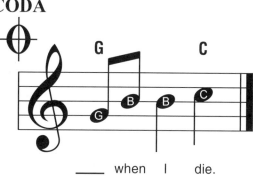

____ when I die.

3 AM

Lyrics by Rob Thomas
Music by Rob Thomas,
Brian Yale, John Leslie Goff
and John Joseph Stanley

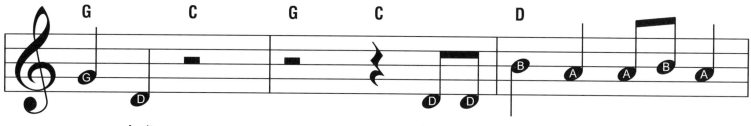

my fault.

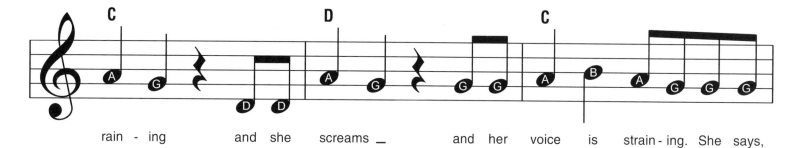

And she on - ly sleeps when it's

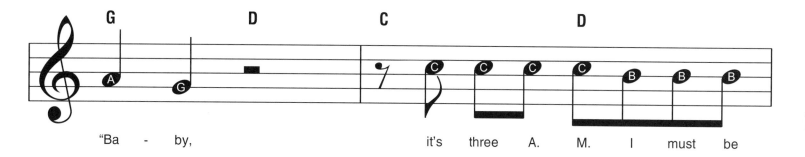

rain - ing   and she screams ___   and her voice is strain - ing. She says,

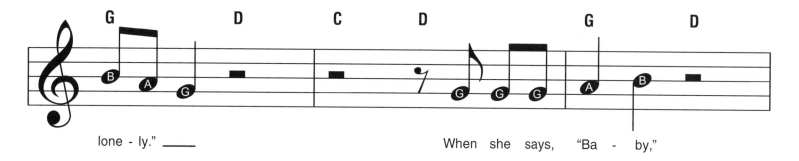

"Ba - by,   it's three A. M. I must be

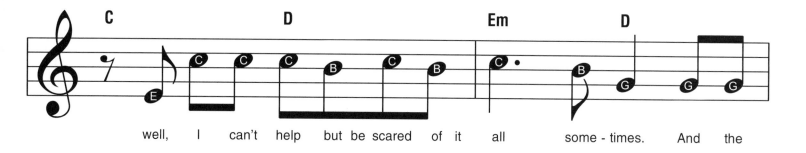

lone - ly." ___   When she says, "Ba - by,"

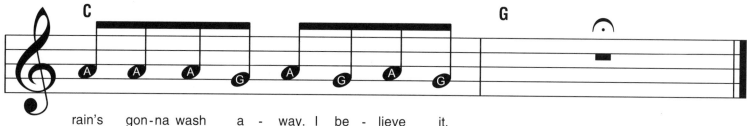

well, I can't help but be scared of it all some - times. And the

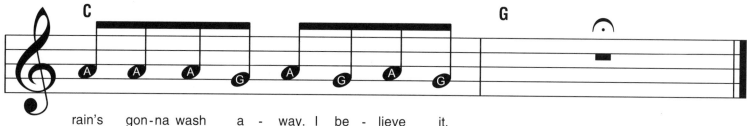

rain's gon-na wash a - way. I be - lieve it.

Toes

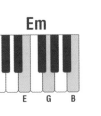
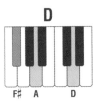

Words and Music by Shawn Mullins,
Zac Brown, Wyatt Durrette
and John Driskell Hopkins

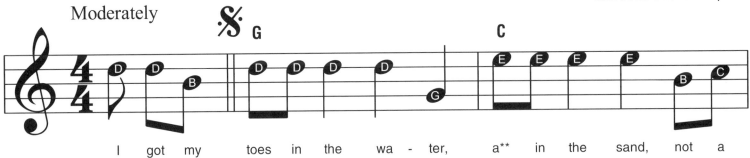

I got my toes in the wa - ter, a** in the sand, not a

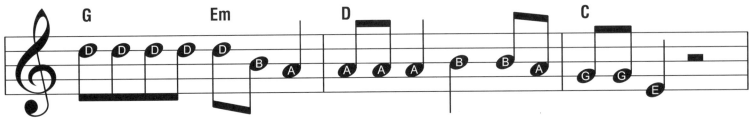

wor - ry in the world, a cold beer in my hand. Life is good to - day,

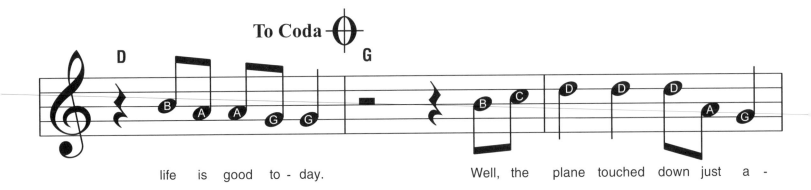

life is good to - day. Well, the plane touched down just a -

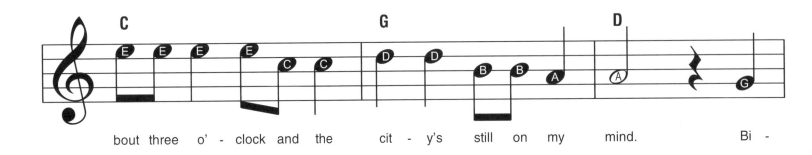

bout three o' - clock and the cit - y's still on my mind. Bi -

Truly, Madly, Deeply

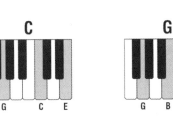
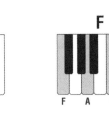
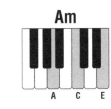

Words and Music by Daniel Jones
and Darren Hayes

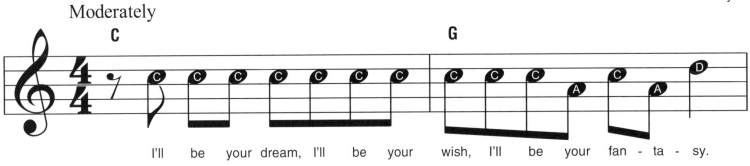

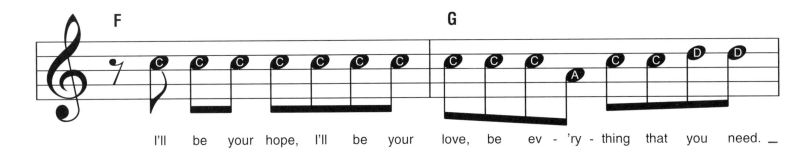

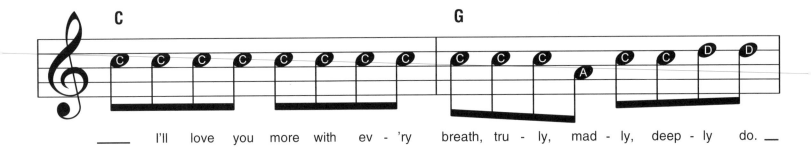

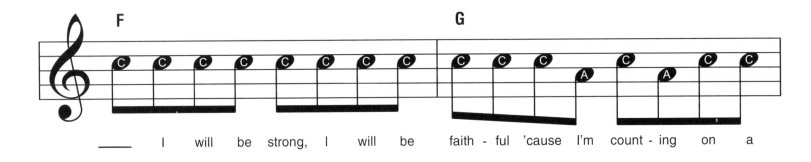

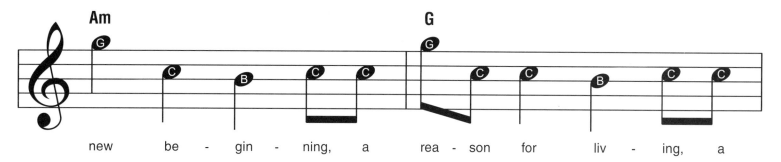

new be - gin - ning, a rea - son for liv - ing, a

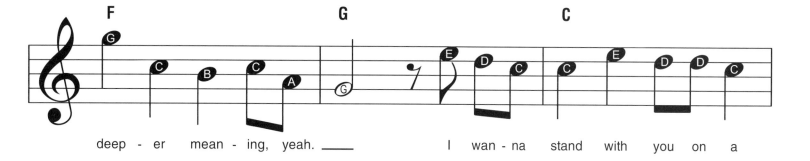

deep - er mean - ing, yeah. _____ I wan - na stand with you on a

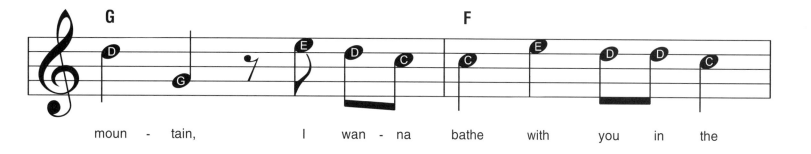

moun - tain, I wan - na bathe with you in the

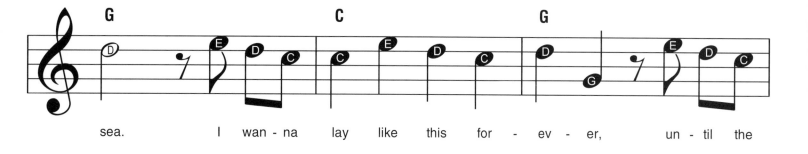

sea. I wan - na lay like this for - ev - er, un - til the

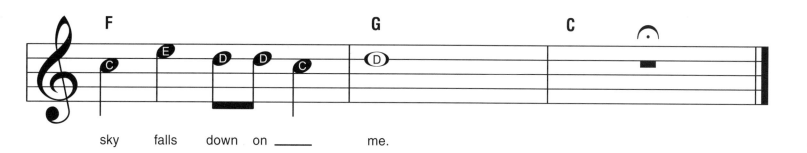

sky falls down on _____ me.

Turn the Page

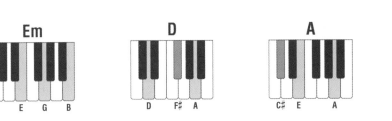
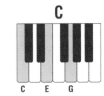

Words and Music by
Bob Seger

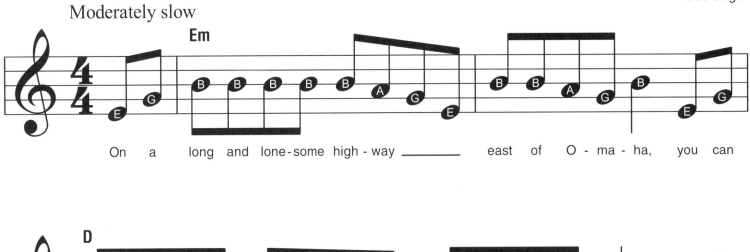

On a   long and lone-some high-way _____ east of O - ma-ha,   you can

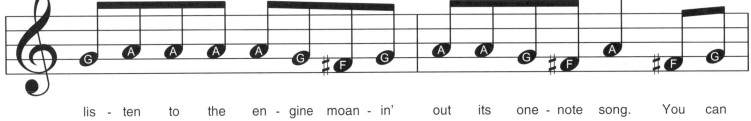

lis - ten   to the en - gine moan-in'   out   its   one - note song.   You can

think   a - bout the wom-an   or the   girl you knew the night   be - fore. _____

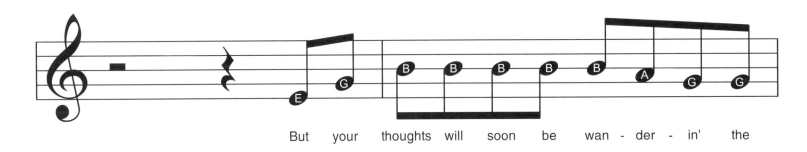

But   your   thoughts will   soon   be wan - der - in'   the

Two Princes

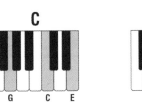
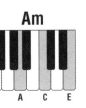
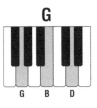
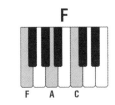

Words and Music by
Spin Doctors

Moderately

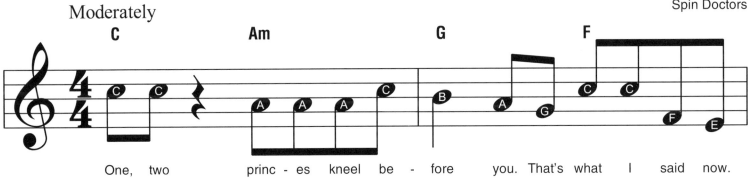

One, two   princ - es kneel be - fore   you. That's what I   said now.

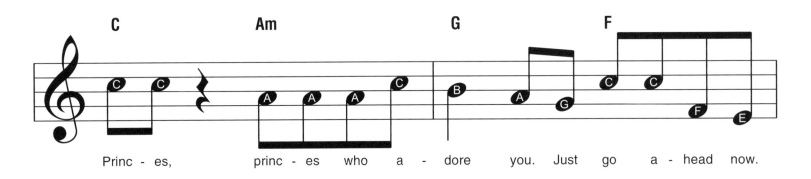

Princ - es,   princ - es who a - dore   you. Just go a - head now.

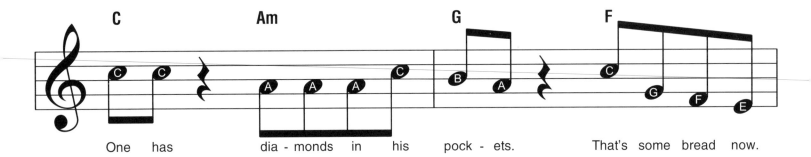

One has   dia - monds in his pock - ets.   That's some bread now.

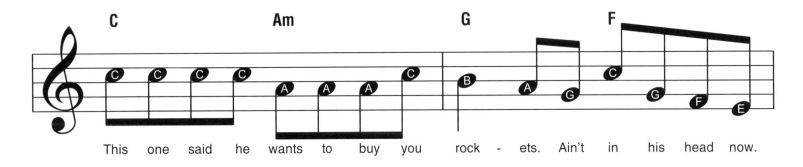

This one said he   wants to buy you rock - ets. Ain't in his head now.

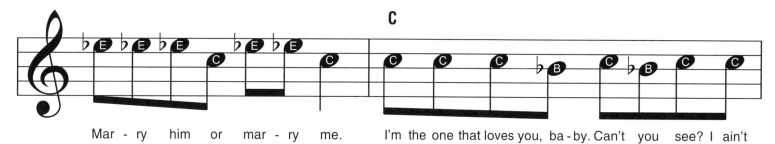

Mar - ry him or mar - ry me. I'm the one that loves you, ba - by. Can't you see? I ain't

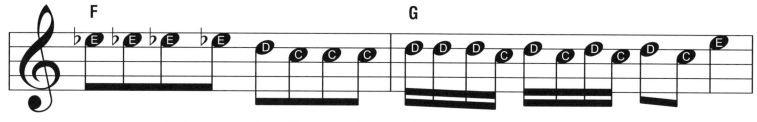

got no fu - ture or a fam - 'ly tree, but I know what a prince and lov - er ought to be.

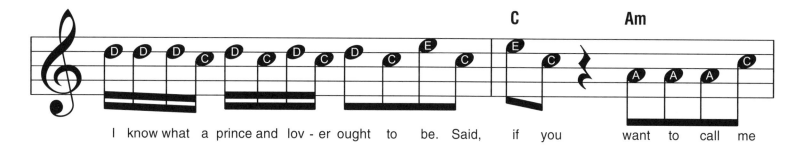

I know what a prince and lov - er ought to be. Said, if you want to call me

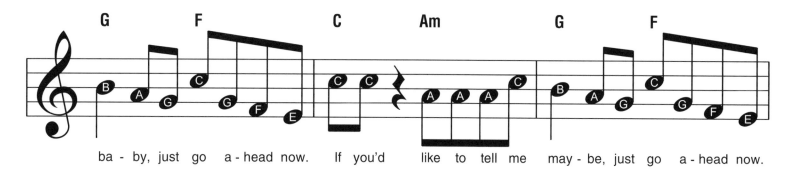

ba - by, just go a - head now. If you'd like to tell me may - be, just go a - head now.

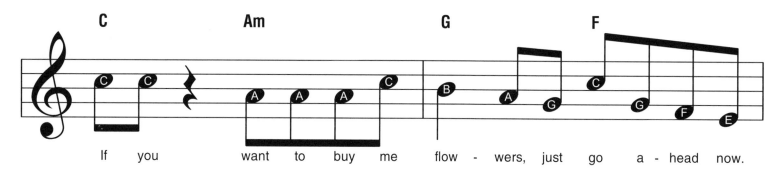

If you want to buy me flow - wers, just go a - head now.

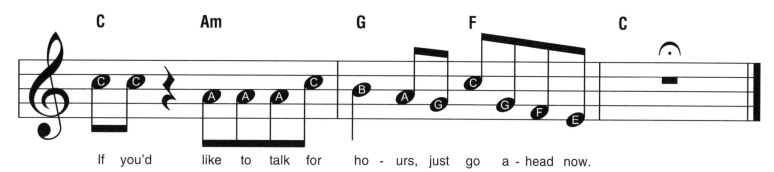

If you'd like to talk for ho - urs, just go a - head now.

Wagon Wheel

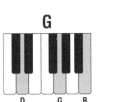 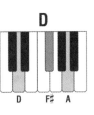 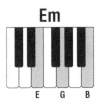 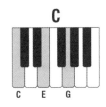

Words and Music by Bob Dylan
and Ketch Secor

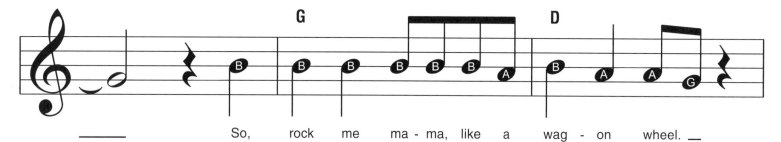

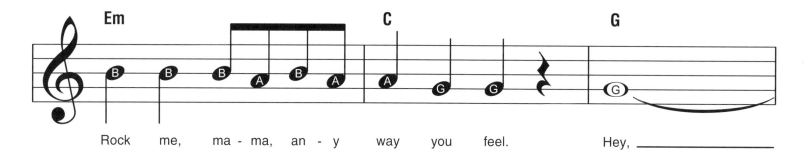

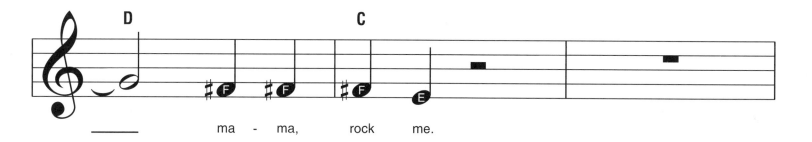

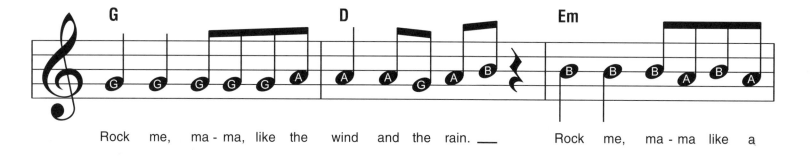

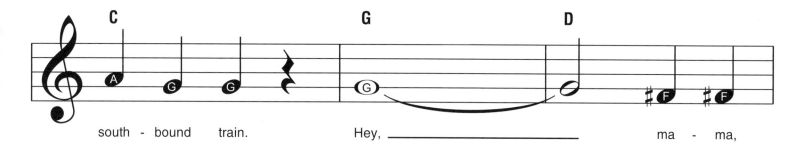

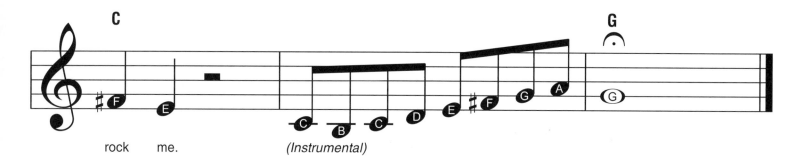

Wake Me Up

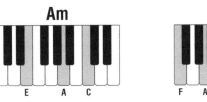 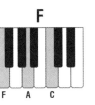 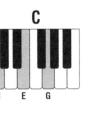 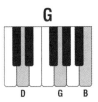

Words and Music by Aloe Blacc,
Tim Bergling and Michael Einziger

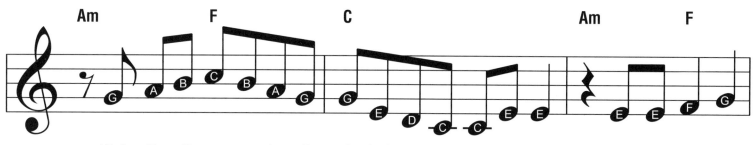

Well, life will pass me by if I don't o-pen up my eyes. Well, that's fine by

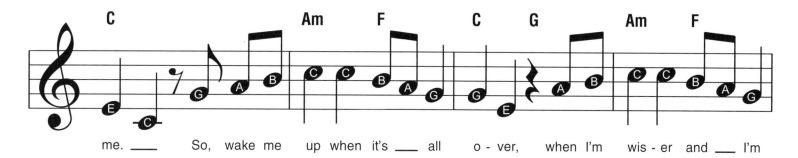

me. ___ So, wake me up when it's ___ all o-ver, when I'm wis-er and ___ I'm

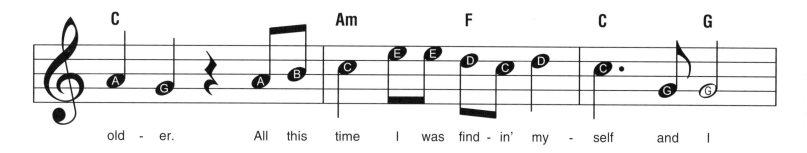

old - er. All this time I was find-in' my - self and I

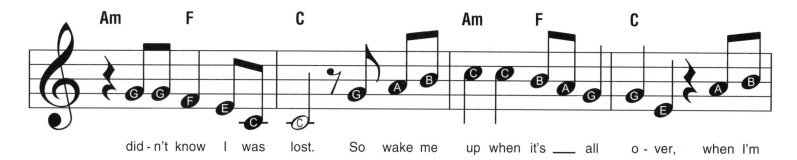

did-n't know I was lost. So wake me up when it's ___ all o-ver, when I'm

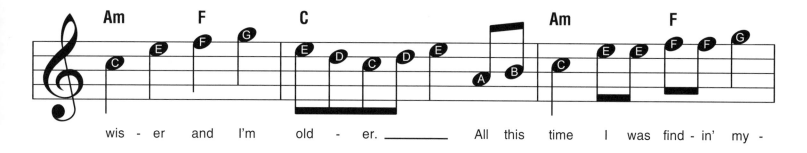

wis-er and I'm old - er. _____ All this time I was find-in' my -

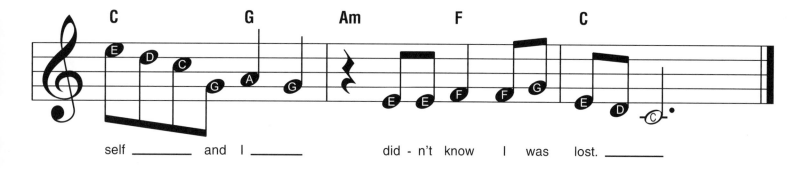

self _____ and I _____ did-n't know I was lost. _____

Wanted Dead or Alive

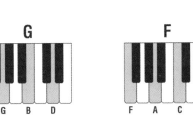
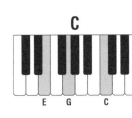
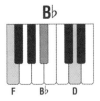

Words and Music by Jon Bon Jovi
and Richie Sambora

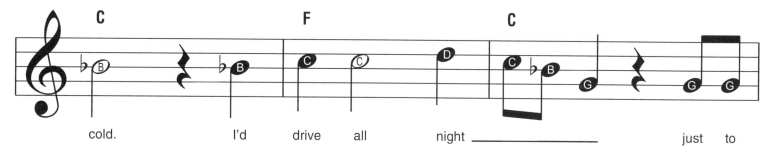

cold. I'd drive all night _____ just to

get back _____ home. _____ I'm a cow - boy,

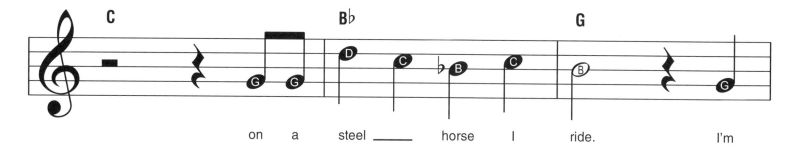

on a steel _____ horse I ride. I'm

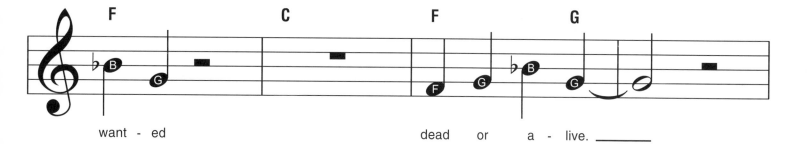

want - ed dead or a - live. _____

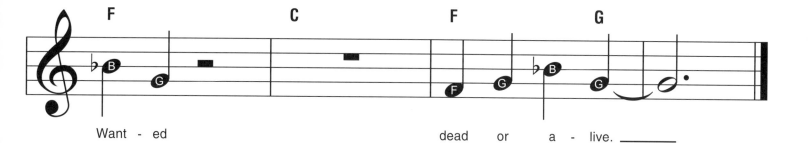

Want - ed dead or a - live. _____

With or Without You

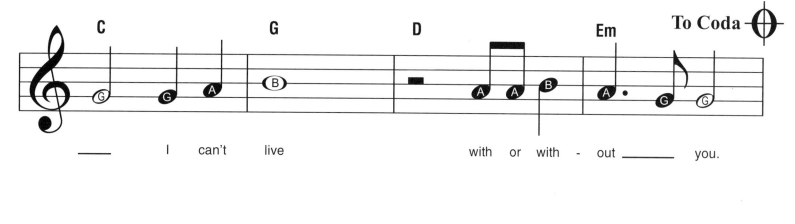

To Coda ⊕

_____ I can't live with or with - out _____ you.

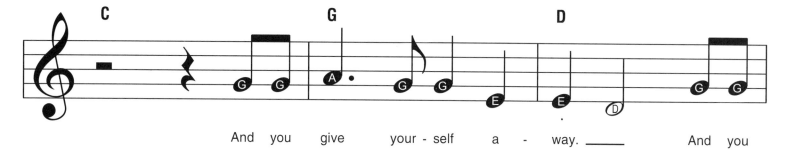

And you give your-self a - way. _____ And you

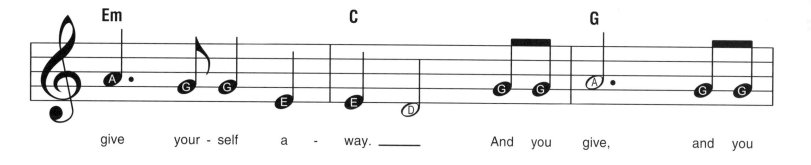

give your-self a - way. _____ And you give, and you

D.S. al Coda
(Return to 𝄋, play to ⊕
and skip to Coda)

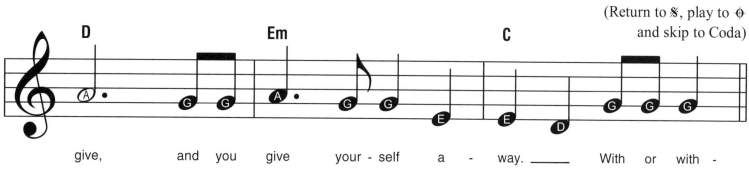

give, and you give your-self a - way. _____ With or with -

CODA ⊕

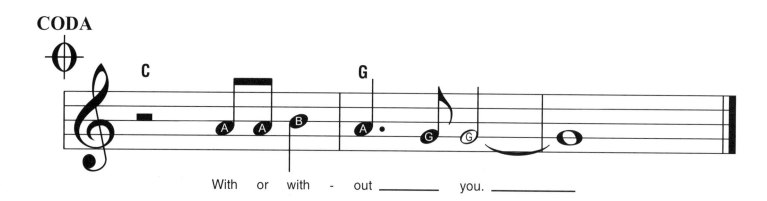

With or with - out _____ you. _____

Wonderful Tonight

Words and Music by
Eric Clapton

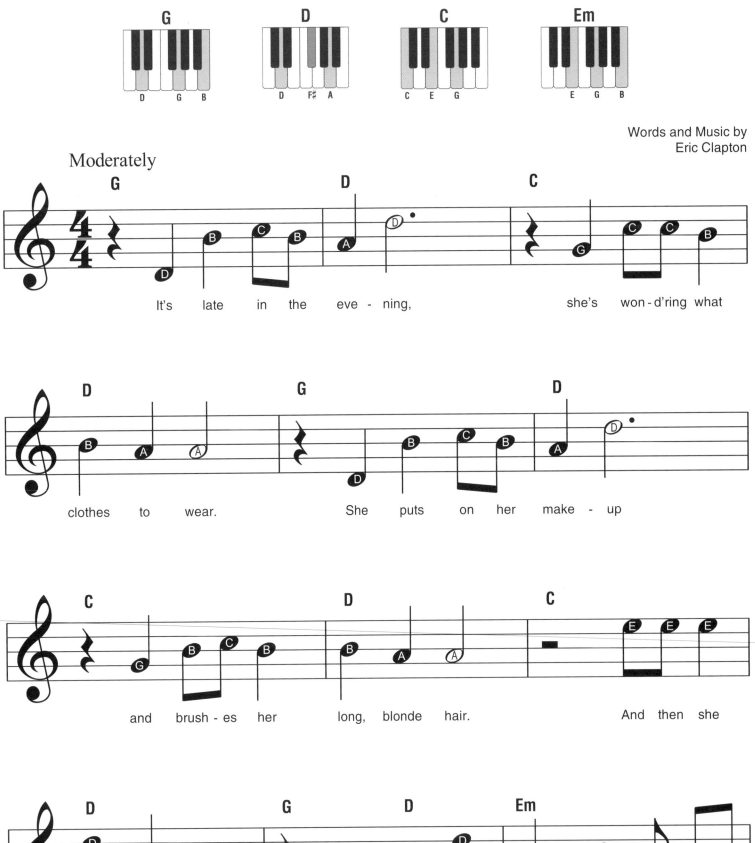

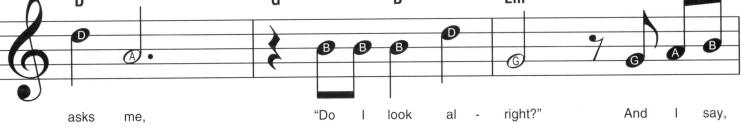

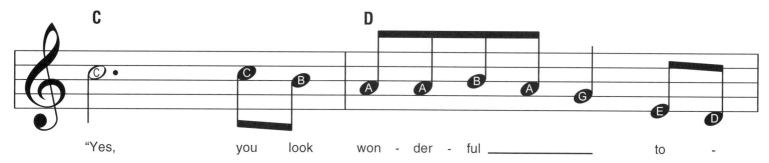

"Yes, you look won - der - ful _____ to -

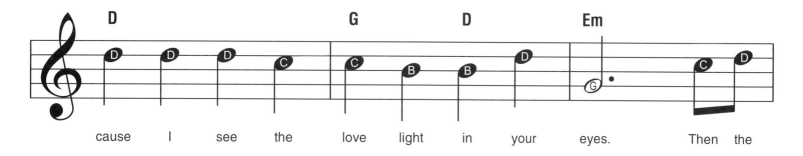

night." I feel won - der - ful be -

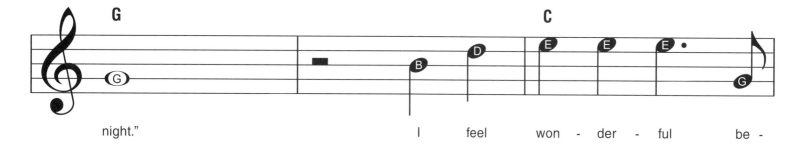

cause I see the love light in your eyes. Then the

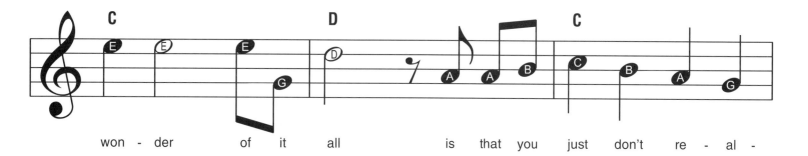

won - der of it all is that you just don't re - al -

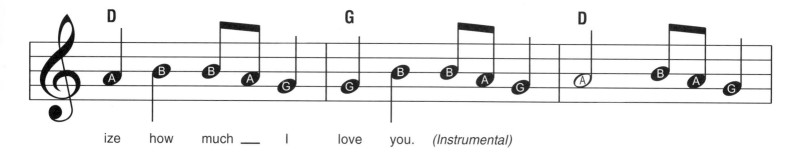

ize how much ___ I love you. *(Instrumental)*

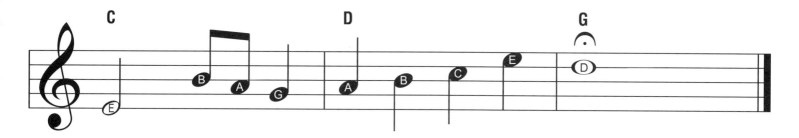

You Raise Me Up

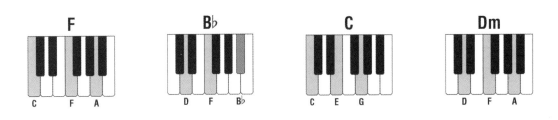

Words and Music by Brendan Graham
and Rolf Lovland

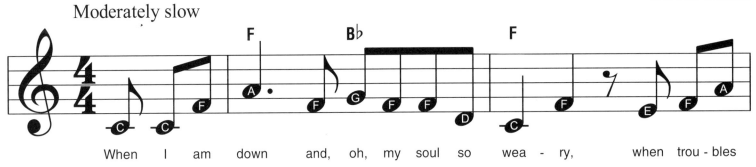

When I am down and, oh, my soul so wea - ry, when trou - bles

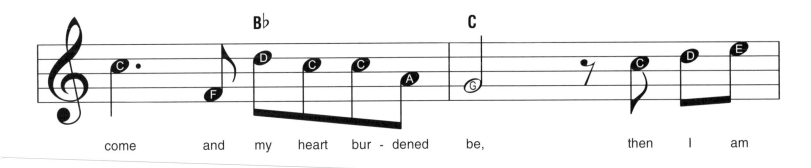

come and my heart bur - dened be, then I am

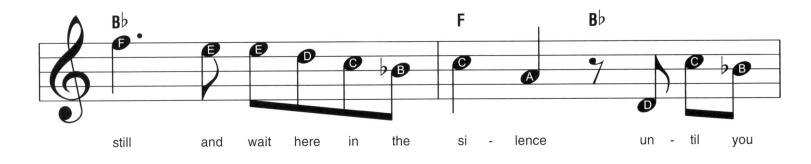

still and wait here in the si - lence un - til you

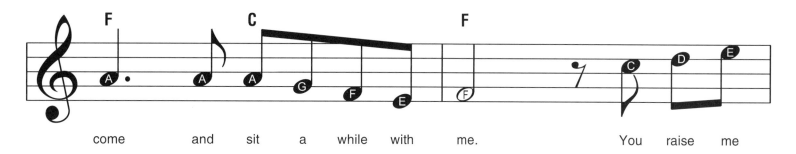

come and sit a while with me. You raise me

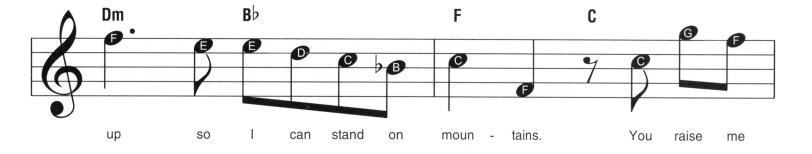

up so I can stand on moun - tains. You raise me

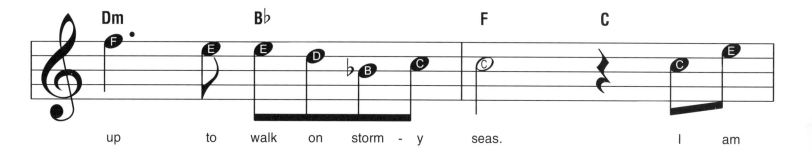

up to walk on storm - y seas. I am

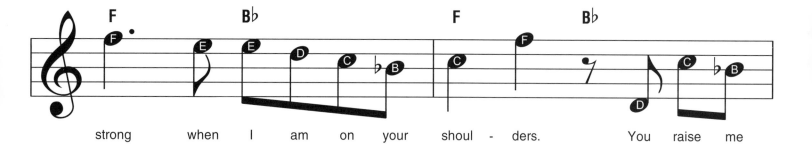

strong when I am on your shoul - ders. You raise me

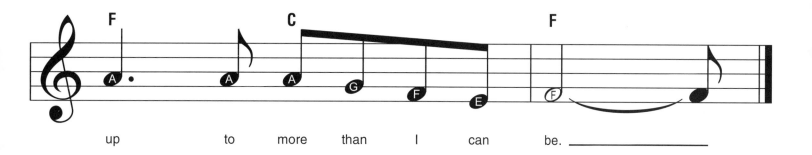

up to more than I can be. _____

You've Got to Hide Your Love Away

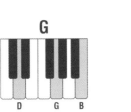
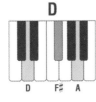
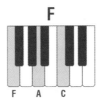
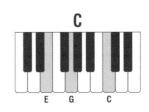

Words and Music by John Lennon
and Paul McCartney

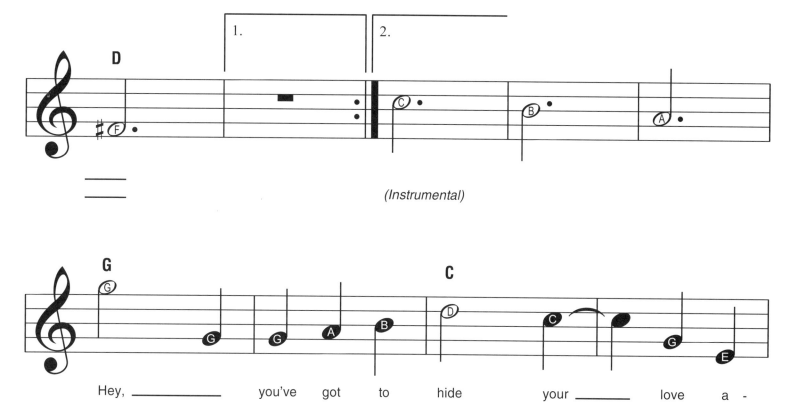

(Instrumental)

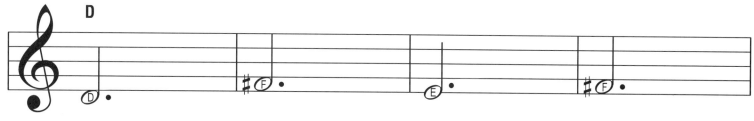

Hey, _____ you've got to hide your _____ love a -

way. (Instrumental)

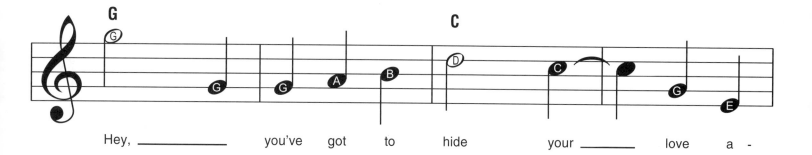

Hey, _____ you've got to hide your _____ love a -

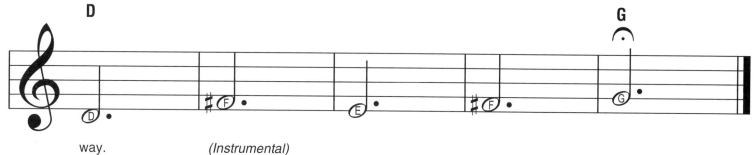

way. (Instrumental)

Zombie

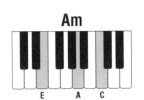
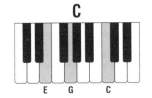
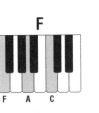
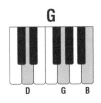

Lyrics and Music by
Dolores O'Riordan

Moderately

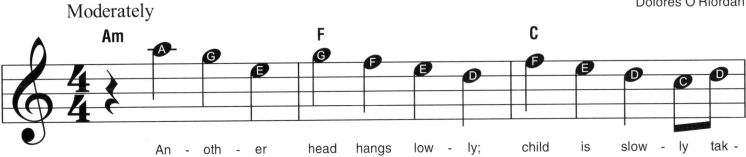

An - oth - er head hangs low - ly; child is slow - ly tak -

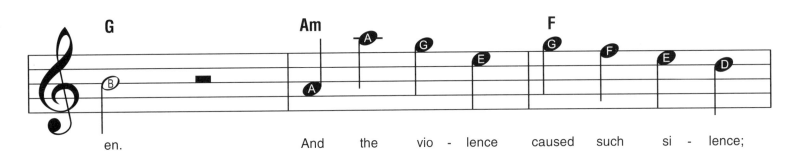

en. And the vio - lence caused such si - lence;

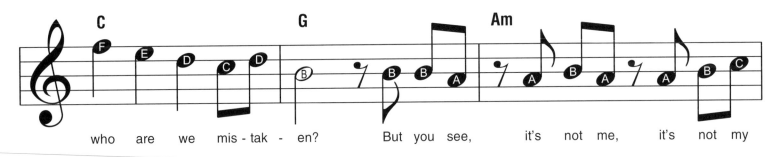

who are we mis - tak - en? But you see, it's not me, it's not my

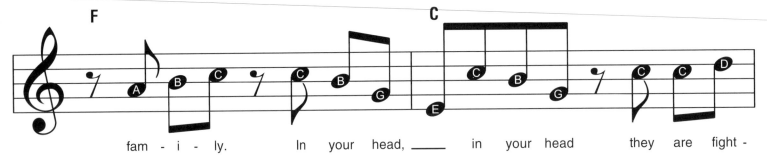

fam - i - ly. In your head, _____ in your head they are fight -

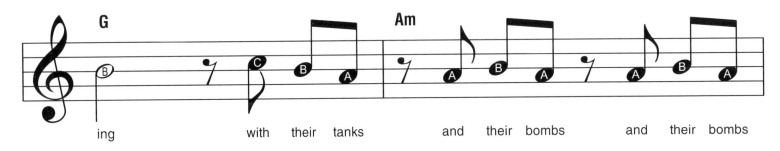

ing with their tanks and their bombs and their bombs

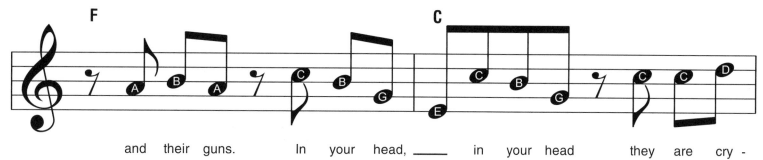

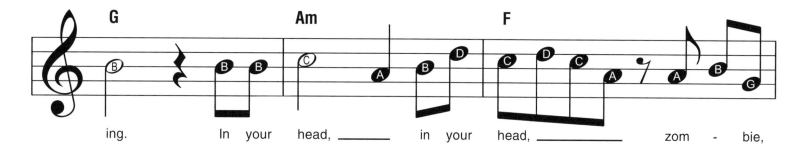

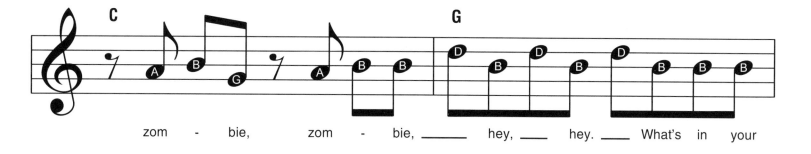

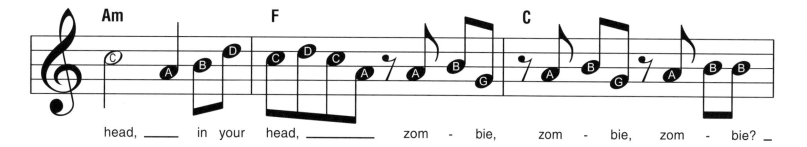

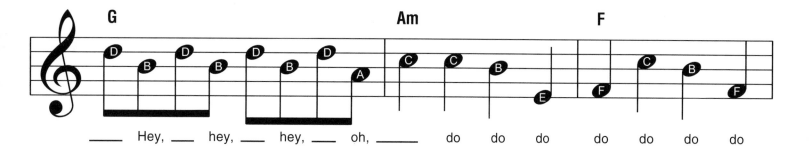

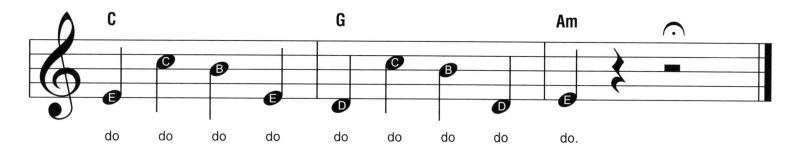

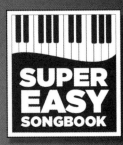

SUPER EASY SONGBOOK

It's super easy! This series features accessible arrangements for piano, with simple right-hand melody, letter names inside each note, and basic left-hand chord diagrams. Perfect for players of all ages!

THE BEATLES
00198161 60 songs......................$15.99

BEAUTIFUL BALLADS
00385162 50 songs......................$14.99

BEETHOVEN
00345533 21 selections................$9.99

BEST SONGS EVER
00329877 60 songs......................$15.99

BROADWAY
00193871 60 songs......................$15.99

JOHNNY CASH
00287524 20 songs........................$9.99

CHART HITS
00380277 24 songs......................$12.99

CHRISTMAS CAROLS
00277955 60 songs......................$15.99

CHRISTMAS SONGS
00236850 60 songs......................$15.99

CHRISTMAS SONGS WITH 3 CHORDS
00367423 30 songs......................$10.99

CLASSIC ROCK
00287526 60 songs......................$15.99

CLASSICAL
00194693 60 selections................$15.99

COUNTRY
00285257 60 songs......................$15.99

DISNEY
00199558 60 songs......................$15.99

BOB DYLAN
00364487 22 songs......................$12.99

BILLIE EILISH
00346515 22 songs......................$10.99

FOLKSONGS
00381031 60 songs......................$15.99

FOUR CHORD SONGS
00249533 60 songs......................$15.99

FROZEN COLLECTION
00334069 14 songs......................$10.99

GEORGE GERSHWIN
00345536 22 songs........................$9.99

GOSPEL
00285256 60 songs......................$15.99

HIT SONGS
00194367 60 songs......................$15.99

HYMNS
00194659 60 songs......................$15.99

JAZZ STANDARDS
00233687 60 songs......................$15.99

BILLY JOEL
00329996 22 songs......................$10.99

ELTON JOHN
00298762 22 songs......................$10.99

KIDS' SONGS
00198009 60 songs......................$15.99

LEAN ON ME
00350593 22 songs........................$9.99

THE LION KING
00303511 9 songs..........................$9.99

ANDREW LLOYD WEBBER
00249580 48 songs......................$19.99

MOVIE SONGS
00233670 60 songs......................$15.99

PEACEFUL MELODIES
00367880 60 songs......................$16.99

POP SONGS FOR KIDS
00346809 60 songs......................$16.99

POP STANDARDS
00233770 60 songs......................$15.99

QUEEN
00294889 20 songs......................$10.99

ED SHEERAN
00287525 20 songs........................$9.99

SIMPLE SONGS
00329906 60 songs......................$15.99

STAR WARS (EPISODES I-IX)
00345560 17 songs......................$10.99

TAYLOR SWIFT
00323195 22 songs......................$10.99

THREE CHORD SONGS
00249664 60 songs......................$15.99

TOP HITS
00300405 22 songs......................$10.99

WORSHIP
00294871 60 songs......................$15.99

www.halleonard.com

Disney characters and artwork TM & © 2021 Disney

Prices, contents and availability subject to change without notice.

0222

327

HAL LEONARD PRESENTS
FAKE BOOKS FOR BEGINNERS!

Entry-level fake books! These books feature larger-than-most fake book notation with simplified harmonies and melodies – and all songs are in the key of C. An introduction addresses basic instruction on playing from a fake book.

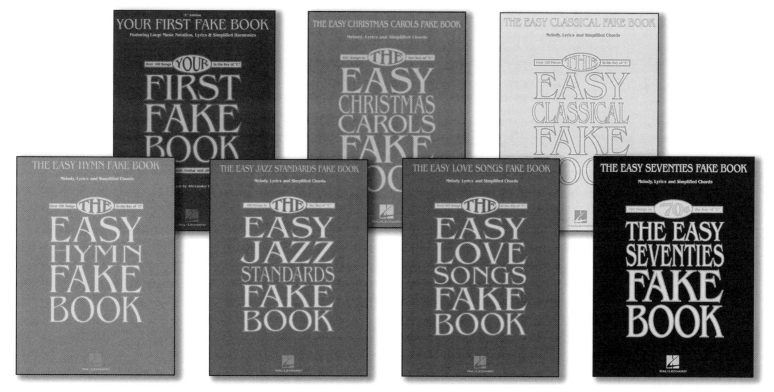

HAL•LEONARD®
halleonard.com

Prices, contents and availability subject to change without notice.

0421
128